Riding with Finesse

How to become a sensitive, elegant and effective rider

by

Val Main MSc

Riding with Finesse

British Library Cataloguing-in-Publication Data
A catalogue record for this book is available from the British Library.

ISBN 978-1-9160531-7-5

Published by PG Print Services Ltd

Paintings © Lynne Barry
Illustrations © Jennifer Pelosi

Cover and layout design by dartworks.design
Layout and proofreading via pgprintandofficeservices.co.uk
Photography of selected paintings by Ken Foulis LBIPP

Printed and bound in Great Britain by Print2Demand Ltd, Westoning

This book is dedicated to my wonderful husband,
who is my proofreader and constant source of support,
and to the horse – a remarkable species:
patient, gentle, affectionate, capable of teaching humanity a
great deal if it is willing to listen.

I would like to acknowledge the debt I owe to Robert Nigel Hall,
FBHS, who was my main source of inspiration.

ACKNOWLEDGEMENTS

Teamwork really did make this dream work. Special thanks to my amazing team: to the super talented artist Lynne Barry who created amazing artworks to complement the book; to Jen Pelosi who created top quality technical drawings; to Paula Good of PG Print and Office Services for proofreading, her guidance throughout the whole process and the fabulous book layout; to Dartworks Design for the cover; to Ken Foulis LBIPP for photographing some of the artworks; to Professor Jo-Anne Murray for her Foreword; and to my husband Doug who proofread and edited the book.

Thanks are also due to my friends, especially Helen MacNeil for being a constant source of support and for putting me in touch with Jen Pelosi. Special thanks are due to Amanda Stears of Edinburgh Veterinary Physiotherapy for proofreading the more technical chapters. Lastly, thanks are due to Sara Hogg for permission to publish pictures of her competing two of our homebred horses, Watherston Arion (the dapple grey Large Riding Horse) on page 98, and Watherston Cassandra (the brown Lightweight Hunter) on pages 51, 64 and 70.

CONTENTS

CHAPTER 3: TRAINING GOALS AND THE HORSE'S BALANCE

CHAPTER 4: THE SEAT

CHAPTER 5: THE HANDS AND THE CONTACT

CHAPTER 6: THE HORSE'S HEAD POSITION AND A PHYSIOLOGICAL EXPLANATION OF CONTACT

CHAPTER 7:
THE RIDING POSITION IN DETAIL

CHAPTER 8: EQUINE MOVEMENT AND WALK TROT AND CANTER

CHAPTER 9: THE THEORY OF THE AIDS

CHAPTER 10: THE AIDS IN DETAIL

CHAPTER 11: THE HALT, THE HALF-HALT AND REIN-BACK

CHAPTER 12: STRAIGHTNESS, BEND, FLEXION AND CIRCLES

CHAPTER 13: LATERAL WORK, TURNS, PIROUETTES AND FULL-PASS

CHAPTER 14: EQUESTRIAN LANGUAGE

FOREWORD BY PROFESSOR JO-ANNE MURRAY

As horse riders, we are striving to improve how we ride and train our horses. There has been a huge surgency in equitation science in recent years whereby scientific methods have been used to evaluate training techniques as well as horse and rider biomechanics. This work helps us better understand how rider biomechanics affect the biomechanics and performance of the horse, and also helps identify what training techniques work and those that are ineffective. This evidence-based approach to riding and training our horses aims to improve their welfare and interactions with us.

Whilst there is a growing body of research into equitation science, the information is not always accessible to the horse rider. For this research to impact the equine community, it needs to be distilled into clear, practical advice that can positively impact the horse.

I am therefore very pleased to write the foreword for this book. Val has invested a huge amount of time and effort into distilling the literature on biomechanics and training into a practical guide for horse riders. This book is an ideal read for the thinking rider who can refer to this book for clarification and inspiration. Also, Val's vision for this book to be positive and inspiring with beautiful illustrations has definitely been achieved. I wholeheartedly applaud Val's efforts to bring scientific knowledge to the equine community for the benefit of educating the rider and improving the welfare of the horse.

ABOUT VAL MAIN

My love for horses was evident from an early age. Even before I could talk, I was gesturing to be lifted on to any and every horse, donkey, or pony. I was truly fortunate to be taught equitation from a very young age at Fulmer School of Equitation, Edinburgh in the 1960s and 1970s. The late Robert Nigel Hall, FBHS, owner of the Fulmer Schools of Equitation, ignited my passion for Classical Riding with his enthusiasm, teaching skills and tales from his time training at The Spanish Riding School in Vienna under the legendary Colonel Alois Podhajsky, the School Director.

The Fulmer Riding Schools offered a differing riding system, which was based on that used at the Spanish Riding School of Vienna. Robert Hall, a visionary, firmly believed that any rider who was willing to work on improving their riding position and their 'feel' could learn equitation and use the finessed aiding system he taught. The focus of his lessons was on the development of feel, the independence of seat and hands and crucially the use of the seat and hands to 'listen to the horse'. My training system is based on my formative years at Fulmer.

A transformative moment in my life was when, aged 12, Robert Hall invited me to have a lesson on his classically schooled Grand Prix level dressage horse, Pepper. The feeling of lightness I experienced when riding the beautifully schooled Pepper exceeded my expectations. Pepper willingly demonstrated how it was possible for a small rider to guide such a large horse with the gentlest of touches and lightest of aids. My ambition from that moment onwards was to one day own and ride horses that were similarly willing and sensitively trained. It was a lesson on so many levels that I will be eternally grateful for.

I have two degrees, both awarded by the University of Edinburgh. In 1980, I graduated with a degree in Psychology, and Biology and in 2005, I graduated with a Master's Degree in Equine Science which I studied at the University of Edinburgh Veterinary School. Thirty years ago, having moved to a small farm in the Scottish Borders, I was able to follow my dream of breeding and training horses. I became actively involved in showing homebred Hunters, Riding Horses and Arabians. Nowadays, my life is spent immersed in horse related activities and reading research papers, particularly in the fields of equine behaviour, equitation science and equine biomechanics. I have competed in Dressage, Showing, Show Jumping and One Day Events. I have been judging Showing classes for 30 years and was invited on to the Arab Horse Society Judging Panel.

My system of riding has as its basis Modern Classical Riding techniques and is enhanced by knowledge of equine biomechanics, learning theory and an understanding of equine memory and intelligence. I currently work as a freelance riding Instructor. In addition to private and shared lessons, I teach a variety of Clinics, both mounted and unmounted.

I also offer a full online service: online mentoring; goal setting sessions and online lessons.

Clinic information is available on my website:

www.valmain.co.uk

MSc Graduation 2005
Left to Right: Val Main / Isobel Duncan / Ruth Harrison

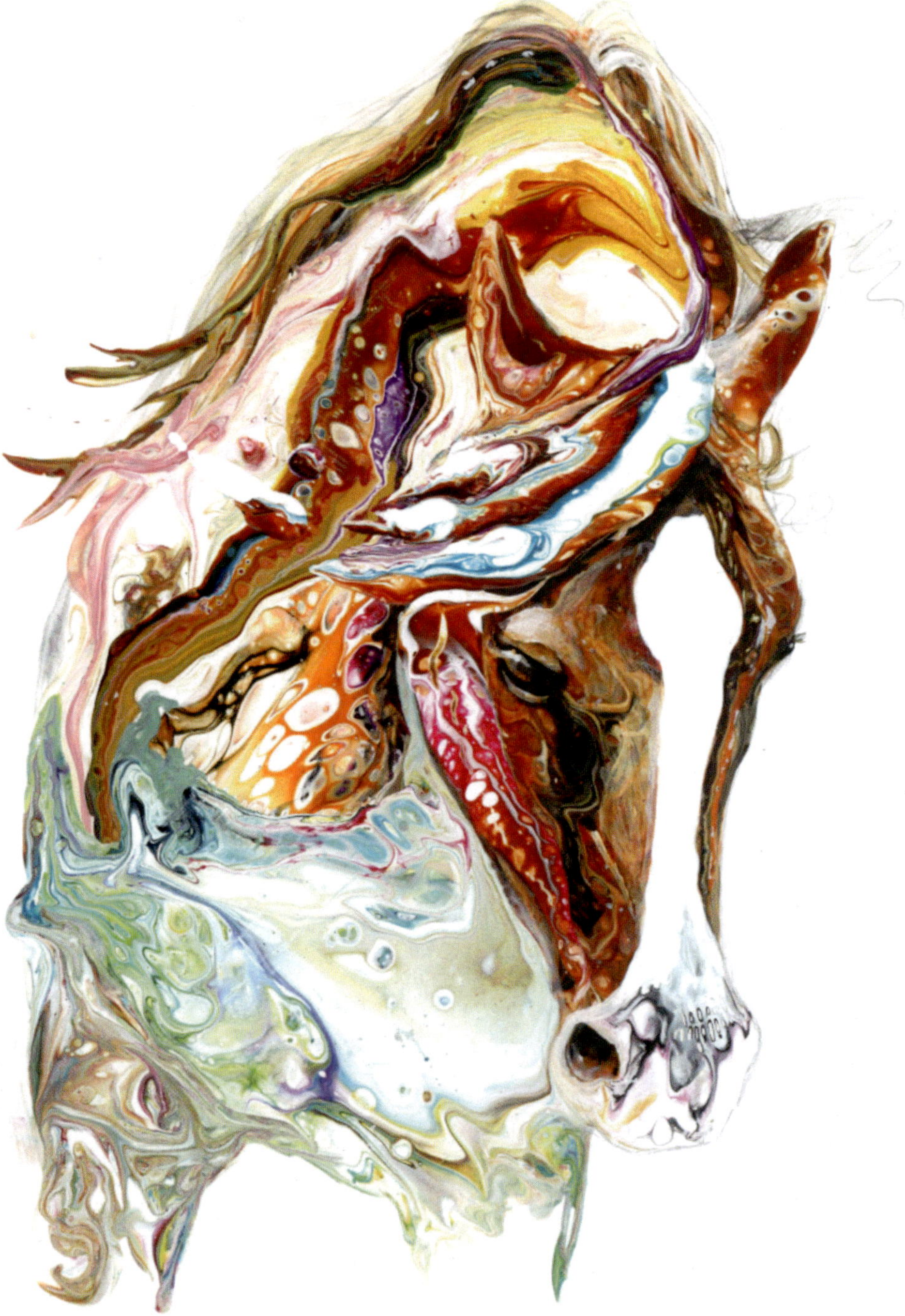

INTRODUCTION

This book contains explanations of how riders can achieve the best possible performance from the horse with the least physical effort… ACHIEVING MORE WITH GREATER EASE. My method is based on a foundation of cooperation between horse and trainer and the making of fair requests of the horse.

This book has been written for anyone, no matter their current skill level, who wishes to become a more skilled and sensitive rider. ANY rider armed with the correct information and with details of subtle riding techniques can develop a more sensitive means of communication with their mount.

Improving the riding position is the starting point. Understanding the functions of a dynamic riding position and how it must work in synchrony with the horse's movements and the aids will enable riders to become more harmoniously connected.

This book will provide all the information needed to enable the reader to become a skilful rider who understands the changes she wishes to bring about in the horse. The rider with an understanding of the horse's natural biomechanics, the theory of the aids, the techniques of their application and knowledge of how to refine the aids down to the smallest movements necessary can train the horse without ever losing the natural beauty of his movements.

Clear communication combined with thoughtful training and light aiding makes the ridden experience more enjoyable for the horse and should harness his desire to co-operate.

FINAL THOUGHTS

It is important never to lose sight of how privileged horse riders are, how wonderful it is to have horses in our lives and how fortunate we are that they will permit us to ride them. It is a magical and very addictive feeling to be totally connected to a horse, to be unaware of anything other than the amazing feeling of harmony with your willing partner, both focused on their private 'conversation'. I hope that this book will enhance your enjoyment of riding and I pray that you never lose the joy and the magic.

A FEW INTRODUCTORY NOTES TO THE BOOK

I hope that I have resisted the urge to make this book too scientifically detailed. I enjoy in-depth scientific explanations but am aware that many in the equestrian community only wish to know how this information can be practically applied to help horses and riders. I have read, absorbed, and cherry-picked the important relevant facts.

For the sake of brevity, I have used the pronoun 'he' when referring to the horse or pony rather than 'he or she' endlessly repeated. I cannot bring myself to use the pronoun it when referring to such beautiful sentient animals.

For clarity, when referring to the rider I have used the pronoun she.

Over the centuries, much equestrian knowledge and best advice has been passed on by word of mouth, thus the origins of some of my favoured quotes are unknown to me but are too useful to be excluded. Where possible, I will attribute the quotes I have used.

Having had many lessons from Robert Hall (FBHS), any quoted sections attributed to him are from memory unless otherwise stated.

MY APPROACH

MY EUREKA MOMENT

Having had the privilege of being present at the birth of a number of foals, I was completely taken aback by how very differently they behaved in the first few hours of birth. Karla was the foal who provided me with my eureka moment. Whilst her hind legs were still in her mother Karicia's birth canal, she was struggling forwards, pulling with her front legs to get free. She appeared to be such a determined little foal. She would not tolerate being guided and supported while she drank, despite being wobbly; she kicked and bucked at anyone who tried to assist. It occurred to me that part of what we attribute to unique personalities (or horsonalities) is, in fact, innate instinctive survival mechanisms. As a prey animal, her instincts were to kick away anything that was holding on to her.

As I watched her make her unsteady progress around the stable, I wondered… WHY ARE HUMANS SO CONFIDENT OF KNOWING THE BEST WAY TO HANDLE HORSES? We prepare ourselves for foaling duty by reading books, and with advice provided by other humans. In those moments, I realised that I had to observe more, question more, and rethink many commonly accepted beliefs.

I had often heard people make comments such as, "Don't let him get the better of you." "If you let him away with it he will know he is the boss now." In my experience, horses do not want to be the boss. They seem calmer and easier to work with when they trust in me and when I am the decision-maker.

Problems occur when horses are pressurised, particularly when they are unsure or confused as to what is being asked of them. Issues also occur when they are not properly prepared for tasks. The less they trust their rider or handler in these situations, the more they will revert to their natural instincts.

There is much emphasis placed on training manners. The horse is required to be polite in his interactions with us, yet he has no concept of what we believe to be polite behaviour. Most horses have good horse-related manners; they know how to interact and coexist with other horses. It is human interaction that can be problematic for them.

Is it possible that using a template based on human values and ideologies is not the best way of handling and training horses? Could a more effective way be to study horse-to-horse interactions and behaviours, and base training methods on an understanding of their instincts and natural behaviours?

COMPELLING HORSES TO DO OUR BIDDING IS NOT THE BEST WAY FORWARD. When compelled, horses usually react in one of two ways, dull subservience, or rebellion. Why are equestrians not focusing on creating more training opportunities where horses can willingly participate in activities, as a partner?

As I watched our foals grow and develop, it became clear to me that horses behaved differently when allowed to develop in an environment in which, within reason, they could express their own wishes. For example, rather than tie horses up to be brushed, they could be allowed to move away if they found a particular brush too hard or too soft and ticklish. It became very apparent that the more we listened to and respected their wishes the more cooperative they became.

Some foals were very confident in new situations whilst others were much more reticent, requiring more patience and support. Some appeared more mischievous and playful than others. I wanted to harness the horse's desire to interact with humans, to retain their interest and cooperation in their training. I recognised one approach would not suit all; each horse had a unique nature and therefore needed a tailored approach in its training if I were to get the best performance from him. This eureka moment laid the foundations for my training sessions, which became more successful and, I believe, more enjoyable for the horses.

TRAINING THOUGHTS

CLARITY AND CONSISTENCY... Clarity and consistency in all interactions with the horse are essential. A good training system must be straightforward to learn and apply, and be easily replicated by all who use it. It must be logical to assist the horse in interpreting it and be functional for reactive and unreactive types alike.

TRUST & PATIENCE... Trust is essential in horse training, hard won and easily lost. All interactions with the horse such as grooming, leading, early handling, groundwork, lunging and long-reining - are the basis on which a relationship of trust is built. Time should be taken to accustom the horse to the equipment riders use. Patience is required with an unfit or newly-backed horse to allow him to build up the necessary strength to carry a rider. All horses should be trained in a gentle and empathetic way, developing confidence that no force will ever be used.

WILLINGNESS... If a rider wishes to establish a sensitive connection with a horse, it is important that she be capable of distinguishing between willingness and tolerance. If the horse is tolerating our interactions rather than engaging with them, it will be much more difficult to build a sensitive connection with him. The horse who does not enjoy his human interactions will often be hard to catch, resistant to bridle or unwilling to approach the mounting block. It is the responsibility of the rider to enlist the horse's cooperation. The goal is that the horse is WILLING to 'accept' the tack and the rider on his back, 'accept the contact' and 'accept the rider's aids'. The key to willingness is fair, gentle, and ethical training. It is important that horses are not forced or pressurised into 'accepting' what we wish of them. They should not be slaves to our will. Requests made of the horse should always be fair and ethical.

PLAYFULNESS... Horses of all ages will indulge in different forms of play, whether in the company of other horses or alone. Horses seek out opportunities for interactive play. The intelligent rider will harness the horse's playful nature, ensuring that the ridden experience is enjoyable for the horse. The enlightened rider will learn to distinguish between activities the horse enjoys and those he will merely tolerate. If the rider pressurises the horse to make rapid progress, the fun will be lost for both.

> "Ask for much, be content with little, and reward often."
> Attributed to Captain Étienne Beudant.

WHY RIDE WITH FINESSE?

The short answer to this question is that it makes the experience pleasanter for the horse. The added advantage of riding with finesse is that the rider can ACHIEVE MORE WITH LESS EFFORT.

Few things are more beautiful than the sight of a horse and rider in perfect balance and harmony – the paces of the horse fluid and rhythmical, the horse moving as if guided by his own thoughts and the rider sitting so still, as if part of the horse. Surely this level of subtle communication is what we all wish for?

The aids originate in the rider's mind. They start with a forethought, an intention. I believe that if any rider understands the changes she wishes to bring about in the horse and has knowledge of how these changes can be achieved the rider will consciously or unconsciously posturally communicate her wishes to the horse.

Horses prefer light aids. The goal is not only to use light aids but gradually to refine them to the smallest movements necessary to effect the desired response. Riders should shy away from descriptions of aids that sound complicated or require them to contort their body to comply with instructions. Each aid should be different combinations of the simple basic instructions.

GET THE BASICS RIGHT AND RIDING ADVANCED MOVEMENTS BECOME MUCH EASIER TO PERFORM

To become harmoniously connected to the horse, a rider must develop a dynamic riding position and be capable of harmonising the aids with the movements of the horse. A rider that has refined their riding position and can remain in dynamic balance is easier to carry.

The aids used must not only be lightly applied but must be carefully timed to influence the horse positively, never blocking nor hindering the natural free-flowing forward movement.

Consistency is essential. The horse must be given time to respond to the aids. Continual repetition of aids results in horses becoming desensitised to the rider's requests and unresponsive.

EACH COMPONENT – THE AIDS, THE HORSES' MOVEMENT AND THE RIDER'S POSITIONS – CAN BE INTERLINKED.

If the desired goal is HARMONY, then each of the three components must move in synchrony. When all three components are working towards the common aim of unity, then rider and horse will seamlessly meld.

If all three components can further impact upon each other positively then the horse will become more fluid and rhythmical and the magic will start to happen.

FEEL AND TACT ARE USEFUL SKILLS

Feel is the rider's ability to react instinctively in a positive manner to the horse's actions.

The development of feel will assist her progress and requires a sensitive, attentive physical connection with the horse. Whilst some riders are more naturally gifted, feel can be taught. The rider with the will, self-discipline, patience, and perseverance to improve her knowledge and apply what she has learned will reap the benefits of her efforts.

Tact in riding is very similar to its counterpart in human interactions. Tact is based upon a deep understanding of horse training practices, riding theory and the nature of horses. A tactful rider is never too demanding, either mentally or physically, of a horse. A tactful rider is patient, self-disciplined, free of ego and attentive to the strengths and weaknesses of each horse.

> "The secret in riding is to do few things right. The more one does, the less one succeeds. The less one does, the more one succeeds."
> Attributed to Nuno Oliveira (1925 - 1989)

RIDING WITH FINESSE: THE AIMS

- TO MAKE THE EXPERIENCE AS PLEASANT AS POSSIBLE FOR THE HORSE
- TO FORM A WILLING AND TRUSTING PARTNERSHIP
- TO ACHIEVE THE BEST PERFORMANCE WITH THE LEAST EFFORT
- TO REFINE THE AIDS
- TO USE ETHICAL TRAINING METHODS
- TO ENCOURAGE THE HORSE TO WORK IN SELF-CARRIAGE
- NEVER TO RESORT TO FORCE
- NEVER TO CREATE AN OUTLINE ARTIFICIALLY

THE SCIENCE

Horses are intelligent and sentient beings that have remarkable memories. The belief that it is necessary to show dominance over a horse in order to train it effectively is at odds with the modern understanding of horses' social nature. Dominance hierarchies, alpha positions, or leadership in social groups are man-made concepts that should not form the basis of any horse training system.

MISTAKES

At some point in their equestrian journey, every rider and trainer will make mistakes. At times they may travel down a path which they consequently realise to be the wrong one. Every rider has moments of recognition and clarity, when they wish they could travel back in time to do things differently. Fortunately, despite having remarkable memories, horses rarely appear to hold our mistakes against us.

PUNISHMENT

> "The horse hasn't read the book on how to ride." Robert Hall

Why inflict punishment on a horse? The use of punishment infers that the horse is wilfully being naughty or uncooperative. What does it achieve? Punishing a specific behaviour does not result in it being forgotten or eliminated, it simply suppresses it.

Much unwanted behaviour occurs when the horse is conflicted, unsure of what is being asked of him or is overexcited. Unwanted behaviours can be reduced by incorporating more groundwork exercises and ensuring training occurs regularly.

If the responsibility for miscommunication is borne by the rider, there should be no need for punishment. The aim of punishment is to stop a behaviour, yet crucially it does nothing to encourage a more acceptable behaviour.

PUNISHMENT IS TOO SIMPLISTIC A SOLUTION FOR DEALING WITH UNWANTED BEHAVIOUR. THE CAUSE OF THE BEHAVIOUR MUST BE CONSIDERED.

AN OVERVIEW OF THE RIDING POSITION

The position a rider adopts will define the scope of her ability to influence the horse. An improvement in the riding position is the starting point for anyone wishing to ride sensitively and effectively. A secure riding position forms a stable base which enables the use of subtle aiding techniques. Instability in the base will affect her ability to resist becoming easily dislodged and resist sudden acceleration or deceleration.

> "If a rider is in the correct position, and the horse was magically removed, they should land on their feet with their knees softly bent."
> Robert Hall.

Small adjustments in the riding position can result in significant improvements in rider stability, an improvement in the connection with the horse and consequently an improvement in his performance. The correct riding position is key to the rider's ability to move in synchrony with the horse. The rider's aim is to be in dynamic balance at all times.

RIDER TIP...

Never force yourself into a riding position that is uncomfortable or painful as this causes excessive postural tension and stiffness.

DYNAMIC BALANCE

The concept of dynamic balance can best be understood by considering what might happen if the horse was magically removed from underneath the rider. If the rider is tipping forwards or in front of the movement she would land on her front. If she is leaning backwards or has fallen behind the movement she will fall on her back.

The horse must balance any load that has been placed upon him and consequently is very sensitive to any variation in a rider's position. If the rider is unstable, moving excessively backwards and forwards or from side to side, she will become an unstable burden. An incorrect riding position makes it difficult, if not impossible, to maintain balance when the horse is in motion.

In the various riding disciplines, riders adopt different positions. For example, in horse racing, a jockey rides with very short stirrup leathers and crouches over the saddle. The jockey lowers their centre of gravity and adopts a position nearer to the shoulders, which enables the horse to balance the rider more easily and thereby achieve greater speeds.

For training and dressage, where speed is not the goal, an upright position has been adopted. Over the centuries this position has hardly changed; the rider sits with a naturally erect posture, the upper body well positioned over the pelvis, and centrally over the seat bones.

THE RIDING POSITION

> "Riding should look effortless; like the swan swimming along in the water there is a lot going on below that cannot be seen."
> Robert Hall

The riding position can be thought of in one of two ways: FORM, the visible appearance; FUNCTION, how it can be used to best effect (this will be set out in later chapters).

THE FORM OF THE RIDING POSITION

The form of the riding position for flatwork training and dressage in essence mirrors the correct standing deportment, with legs apart and knees softly bent.

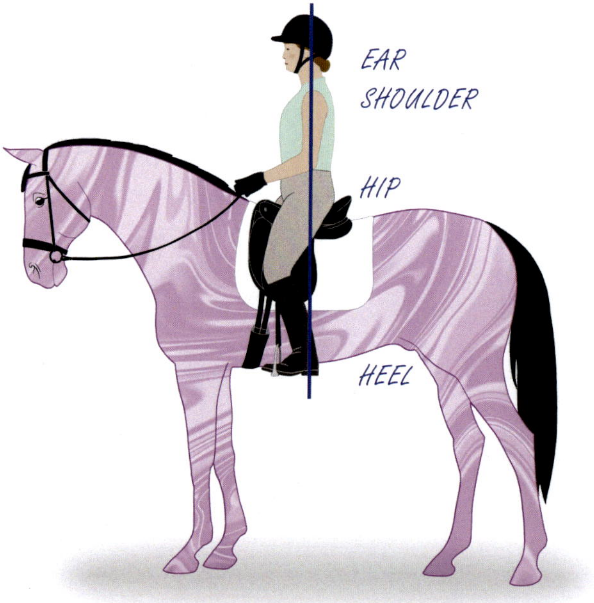

RIDER TIP...

To check your position, ask "What would happen if the horse was magically removed from under me? Would I land on my feet, back or front?"

The correct riding alignment is:

EAR, SHOULDER, HIP AND HEEL IN VERTICAL ALIGNMENT.

The closer the rider can align herself to the correct position, the more easily she can develop the functionality of her riding position. A measure of a rider's skill is her ability to inconspicuously influence and aid the horse whilst seamlessly harmonising her movements.

The heart of the riding position is good posture and body symmetry. The rider wishing to become elegant should work at eliminating poor movement patterns, poor balance, and poor posture. The development of sufficient flexibility and strength will stabilise the riding position and enable synchronous movement with the horse.

DEVELOPING FEEL

> "The horse knows how to move, and it is the rider's job to let it move."
> Robert Hall.

Feel describes the rider's ability to predict and instinctively react to the horse's actions. Body awareness, good balance and reactive body control are the prerequisites in developing feel.

It takes many hours of practice to enable a rider to develop sensitive feel. This development will occur more rapidly if the rider is in the correct riding position and in a relaxed state of mind.

An important aspect of feel is an ability to know which leg or legs the horse will move next. The leg sequence of the horse's gaits have a predictable pattern; knowledge of this enables the fine timing of aids.

With increasingly sensitive feel the rider develops the ability to predict the exact moment a horse will transition from one gait to another. This ability enables her to retain good balance throughout the process of the transition.

The rider who can more easily predict the horse's movements is capable of more subtle timing of her aids and influences.

RIDER TIP...

Establishing a good rhythm in all paces will greatly assist in the development of feel.

FACTORS THAT AFFECT THE RIDING POSITION

- THE SADDLE
- RIDER SYMMETRY AND BALANCE
- THE HORSE'S BALANCE
- RIDER WEIGHT AND FITNESS LEVEL
- RIDER MENTAL STATE AND POSTURAL TENSION
- STIRRUP LENGTH

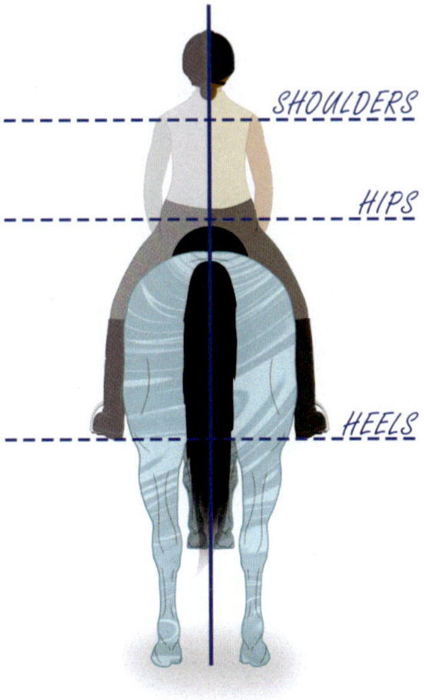

THE SADDLE... Saddle fit can be a problematic issue. The saddle should fit both rider and horse, but the best possible fit may be a compromise. Some horses have conformational issues which create difficulties for good saddle fit. Some may stand high behind the saddle and low at the front. Other horses may have a very high wither which tilts the saddle and concentrates pressure on the horse's back. The location of the horse's girth groove relative to the rear of his shoulder blade can also create problems for saddle fit and stability.

It is impossible to maintain a good position if the saddle is not well designed and correctly balanced. The rider's seat is the primary means by which they communicate with the horse. When a saddle is the correct length, the rider should be able to fit her hand between the cantle and her buttocks. If the saddle is too small, her seat will not be correctly aligned.

The rider should sit in the deepest part of the saddle, which should provide a level surface under the seatbones. When correctly balanced, most modern saddles are designed to sit with the cantle higher than the pommel. A pommel sitting level with or higher than the cantle usually indicates incorrect balance. If the saddle is not correctly balanced, the rider must physically compensate to retain their balance. This can be the cause of positional instability, discomfort, tipping, or leaning.

The saddle must also permit her to place sufficient leg length against the horse. The thigh and knee blocks should provide appropriate support without locking her in place. The stirrup bars should be positioned to assist the rider's vertical alignment; her feet should be under her centre of gravity.

The saddle should function by distributing the rider's weight evenly over a large surface, providing a stable base that does not rock backwards or forwards, nor slip from side to side. The saddle should be the correct size for the horse, not extending beyond the horse's last rib onto his lumbar area. As a rough guide, the front aspect of the tree should be placed two fingers' width behind the back of the horse's shoulder blade. Pressure on or against the shoulder blade restricts foreleg movement, causing discomfort, and may negatively affect the horse's rhythm and balance.

The saddle is positioned over the top of the horse's ribs and rests on his back muscles. The gullet of the saddle should be sufficiently wide to avoid placing pressure on the horse's spine. The tree, tree bars and panels must conform to the shape of the horse's back to prevent rocking, rubbing, or slipping. It must not bridge, create pressure points nor pinch.

Regular visits from a qualified saddle fitter are recommended to assess the saddle's fit and balance. Most horses change shape seasonally and as they develop the correct musculature.

RIDER SYMMETRY AND BALANCE... Just as the horse takes time to develop symmetrical body strength and flexibility, the rider must also focus on developing good symmetry. The rider's weight should be positioned centrally, equally over both seat bones and distributed evenly over both sides of the saddle. The rider should resist collapsing, dipping, or tipping at the waist. If the rider is unable to keep their weight centrally over the horse, their position will be very unstable, and they will struggle to maintain dynamic balance.

THE HORSE'S BALANCE... There undoubtedly exists a significant interaction between the horse's balance and the rider's balance; either party can assist or hamper the other Horses vary significantly in their natural balance and their ability to carry a rider easily; some give an uphill feeling; others travel on the forehand. Some horses become unbalanced when turning, circling, or transitioning to a different gait. A very unbalanced horse will have a significant detrimental effect on the rider's balance and position.

RIDER WEIGHT AND FITNESS LEVEL... Considering two riders of similar height and ability, one being heavier than the other, it is easier for the horse to carry the lighter rider. However, there is a maximum weight that each horse can carry and balance easily. When that limit is exceeded the horse will struggle to move rhythmically and may become prone to tripping and injury.

A rider who lacks flexibility and fitness will struggle to remain in balance. Riding does require muscular effort. Anyone who takes a riding lesson after a period out of the saddle will be aware of the muscles that were used. Riders can improve their fitness level, balance, and stability with targeted unmounted exercises, and should be sufficiently exercise tolerant not to become breathless when riding.

RIDER MENTAL STATE AND POSTURAL TENSION... The rider's mental state can have a significant effect on breathing rate, breathing depth, and muscle tension. Fear and anxiety can cause shallow breathing, holding of breath and excess body tension. Excess body tension will prevent the rider from moving in synchrony with the horse.

Conversely, over-relaxation is not advisable as at the heart of the correct riding position is good posture. Such a relaxed state can cause slouching, a heavy seat, and will inhibit free-flowing forward movement.

Despite its military origins, the correct riding position has many more similarities with the posture, movements, fluidity, and strength of a dancer than the stiff military posture.

STIRRUP LENGTH... Finding the optimum stirrup length will greatly assist the rider's leg position and overall balance. Short stirrups can push the rider's seat out of the deepest part of the saddle, towards the cantle. If the stirrups are overly short, the rider's knees may travel over the knee rolls, rotating them outwards, which in turn positions the heel inwards.

When riding with stirrups which are too long, the rider will constantly be reaching for the irons, often losing her stirrups, and resorting to gripping in an attempt to stabilise her legs.

For flatwork, which involves rising trot, the correct stirrup length can be found by relaxing the legs and feet out of the stirrup irons. If using traditional stirrup irons, the bottom of the iron should fall roughly at the ankle. If using irons designed to assist with shock absorption which have a thicker tread, the bottom of the iron should fall below the ankle.

When the stirrup length is correctly adjusted, the foot should slip easily into the irons by turning the toes up. Another good measure of correct stirrup length is that, when standing, the rider should clear the saddle by roughly 4 inches.

These are general rules; however, other factors such as the length of the rider's legs or the shape of the horse's ribcage may require the lengthening or shortening of the stirrups.

When jumping, the stirrups are usually shortened by 2 or 3 inches.

NATURAL TENDENCIES TO AVOID

Humans have certain natural tendencies which will hinder riding progress. Accomplished riders have trained themselves to resist them. Different riders are affected to differing degrees by these predispositions…

THE BODY'S INSTINCTIVE RESPONSE TO ADOPT THE FOETAL POSITION… When overly anxious, becoming unbalanced or when the horse unexpectedly spooks or spins, the foetal position is a natural instinctive protective reaction. In this position, by curving the back, bending, and drawing the head and limbs towards the torso, the neck, brain, and vital organs are protected from injury.

For some riders this becomes a significant issue when their riding confidence is low. Even a small tendency towards the foetal position will result in positional insecurity. When the rider's legs close and grip upwards, her seat will lose contact with the saddle. Tension in the lower back and the loss of the lumber curve will render her less able to absorb the horse's movement, ultimately causing her to bounce in the saddle. A vicious circle of increasing insecurity and greater anxiety levels commences.

TRYING TOO HARD… Trying too hard and overriding are counterproductive, ultimately resulting in tiredness, which will negatively impact upon balance and position. Overriding will not assist in building a cooperative and harmonious relationship with a horse. It is useful to make notes and reflect after each training session. In life we are often advised that the route to success lies in hard work. In reality, to become successful 'working smarter not harder' is often more effective.

MANUAL DOMINANCE… Humans are naturally manually dominant. The rider should resist this inclination and preferentially use her seat to aid the horse where possible rather than the hands. The hands should be used as lightly and as infrequently as is possible.

TRAINING GOALS AND THE HORSE'S BALANCE

In order to carry the rider the horse must adjust his natural way of going and his biomechanics. It is therefore helpful to understand the impact the rider has on the horse's natural movement and balance. The rider aims to preserve the natural beauty of the horse's movements and to help the horse in the development of the strength necessary to carry her with greater ease.

It is wise to have a good grasp of training goals, clear expectations of the time required to achieve them and a plan for progress. If a rider is clear in her mind as to which aspects of a horse's natural movements she would like to preserve and which she would like to adjust, she will make more rapid training progress. Clarity of intention permits precise and consistent communication with the horse. Horses can be rapid learners; they gain confidence from a confident rider.

THE BASIC AIMS IN TRAINING...

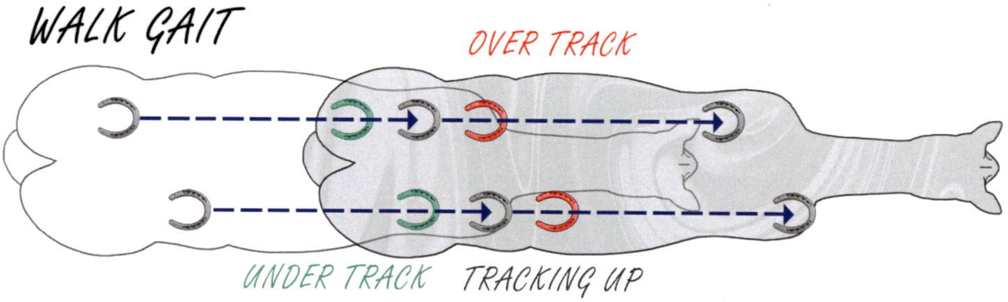

TO PRESERVE FREE FORWARD MOVEMENT... The horse that has never been ridden will move freely forwards. The rider in a good position and in dynamic balance will not hinder the horse in freely traveling forward in rhythm.

TO ENCOURAGE OVERTRACKING... The rider should be aware of the horse's steps and where they land so that she can assist the horse in tracking up. Further, he should be encouraged to develop the strength to over-track. If the horse is not tracking up, this indicates that he is not using his hind quarters and back correctly.

TO ENCOURAGE LIFTING OF THE BACK... The horse's spine can be compared to a beam which has support at each end. Unlike a wooden beam, the horse's 'beam' has a slight natural dip in the middle and the horse's spine compresses when weight is placed upon it. The additional weight of a saddle and rider in this region, which does not have direct support, increases the hollowing tendency.

The rider should encourage the horse to make a bridge of his back and resist any tendency to hollow. This is achieved by encouraging the horse to step well under his body, especially in half-halts and halts.

TO TRAVEL STRAIGHT AND TO ENCOURAGE SUPPLENESS... The horse is encouraged to develop symmetrical body balance through correct training.

TO DEVELOP STRENGTH, THE HORSE'S FRAME SHOULD BE ENCOURAGED TO LENGTHEN AND SHORTEN, BEND AND FLEX GYMNASTICALLY TO DEVELOP SYMMETRICAL BODY BALANCE.

THE HORSE'S BALANCE

The horse's natural movement involves exerting instinctive control over the opposing forces of the hind limbs and the forelimbs. The powerful hindlimbs thrust the horse forwards. This thrust has a rotational element which has the tendency to drive the horse in to the ground. The forelimbs resist the rotational element and redirect the thrust uphill, thus preventing the horse from becoming destabilised.

Horses which have not been ridden are rarely observed to be traveling on the forehand. Feral horses appear graceful and will naturally perform movements such as extended trot, extended canter and passage.

The horse has evolved to run and turn quickly as a means of surviving predator attacks. When startled the horse can engage the muscles that assist the lightening of the forehand which enables him to take flight easily and increase the manoeuvrability of his forehand.

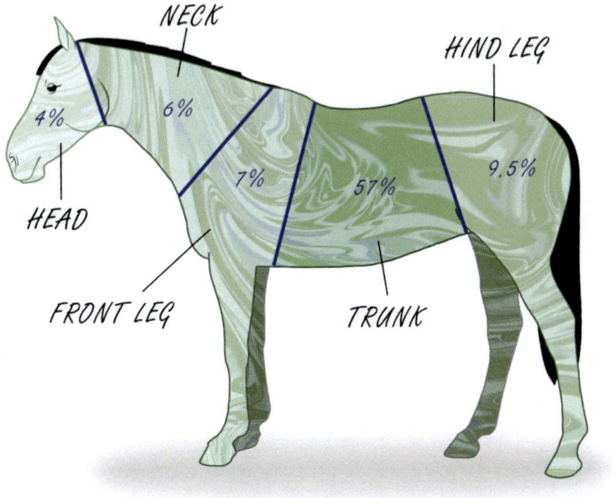

The parts of the horse, expressed as a % of overall weight.

THE HORSE'S CONFORMATION

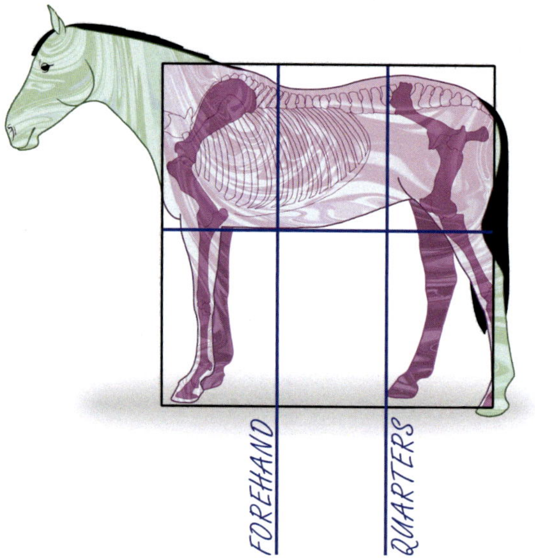

The horse's conformation plays a crucial role in the quality of his movement and in how easily he can lighten his forehand. Some breeds of horse are naturally more athletic and generally give a more uphill feeling. The neck set is an important factor in this: the higher neck set is more easily balanced than the lower neck set. If a horse's withers are lower than his hindquarters, his balance has a natural inclination to be downhill. The horse with withers which sit higher than his hindquarters will tend towards a more uphill balance.

A tried and tested way of assessing the overall symmetry of a horse's conformation is to consider him with reference to a square. The horse's torso and legs should fit in to a square. The forehand, middle and hindquarters should each be one third of the horse's length. If a horizontal line is drawn below the breastbone, the distance from the breastbone to the withers should be equal to the distance from the breastbone to the ground.

The trained horse should always have an uphill balance.

TURNING

The horse's forelimbs are attached and supported purely by a network of muscles, tendons and ligaments. The scapula does not have a bony connection to the torso, which permits greater scapula mobility. The scapula itself is capable of significant rotation and can move up, down, forwards and backwards across the rib cage. The horse naturally turns by bringing his inside foreleg underneath his body, leaning in on the turn and pushing to generate a turning force.

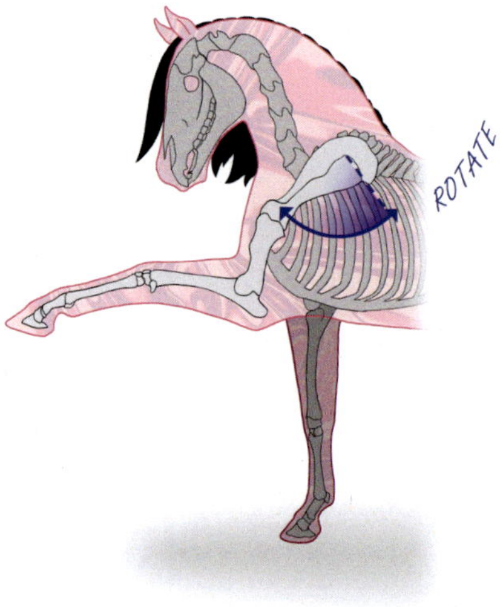

Under saddle, the untrained horse cannot perform correctly balanced circles. The horse should be trained progressively to bear weight on the outer forelimb when turning, which is the opposite of his natural tendency. Eventually, he will carry weight evenly over the forelimbs which greatly assists his horizontal balance.

THE THORACIC SLING

The ribcage is suspended between the forelimbs by means of a muscle sling, called the thoracic sling. The muscles of the sling are attached to the cervical vertebrae, the ribcage and behind the scapula. The Serratus ventralis muscle is the largest of the muscles which support the chest. It is comprised of 2 neck (cervical) and 2 chest (thoracic) sections.

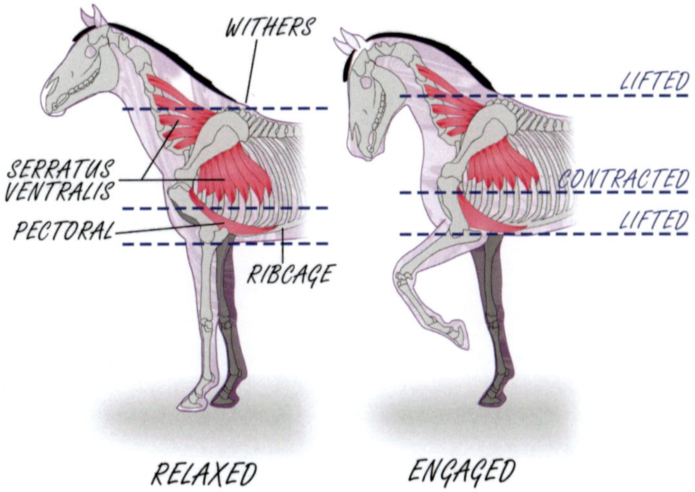

When the sling muscles are contracted (engaged), the horse's withers lift. This results in the horse becoming taller. When these muscles are relaxed, the withers lower and the horse may travel on his forehand.

Equal strength in the left and right sling muscles holds the horse's ribcage centrally. These muscles also function to stabilise the ribcage and maintain horizontal balance in movement when a forelimb is lifted.

RIDER EFFECT ON THE NATURAL MOVEMENT

The weight of the saddle and rider is sited nearer to the forehand. This results in the horse's forehand being required to perform more of the lifting work associated with carrying the rider. When standing, the horse naturally carries around 55% of his weight over his forehand.

The increased burden on the forehand causes most newly backed horses to have a tendency towards travelling on the forehand. It takes time for the horse to develop the necessary strength to travel in an uphill manner when carrying the rider.

The aim in training is to lighten the forehand to improve balance and facilitate responsive control of the forehand as a heavy forehand lacks manoeuvrability and adjustability.

TO DEVELOP UPHILL BALANCE IN THE HORSE, THE RIDER SHOULD DEVELOP STRENGTH IN THE MUSCLES OF THE THORACIC SLING TO LIFT THE FOREHAND DURING RIDDEN SESSIONS.

THE NEXT STAGE IN TRAINING

As training progresses the rider aims to preserve the basic aims of training in addition to developing the following characteristics:

IMPROVED BALANCE... Through training the horse's centre of gravity is encouraged to move towards the haunches. This does not result in the combined weight of horse and rider being distributed equally over the front and the back limbs. The forelimbs will always bear the greater burden.

FORWARDNESS... The rider should train the horse to become forward. Forwardness is not related to how fast the horse is moving but is concerned with preserving responsiveness and the horse's desire to work forward in a balanced rhythm. Any increase in speed before the horse has developed sufficient strength and balance results in 'rushing'.

RHYTHM... The natural rhythm of the gaits should be preserved. The rider should guard against rushing or pushing the horse significantly out of his natural rhythm which may result in him falling on to the forehand and losing balance.

CORRECT CONTACT... With the development of better balance the rider can improve the lightness of the contact.

RELAXATION... With more training and the development of trust, the horse becomes more relaxed in training sessions. This is achieved by good preparation for the task involved. Humans and horses alike must be mentally relaxed to be physically relaxed. The rider's responsibility is to approach each training session with the correct mindset to assist the horse in his relaxation.

CONNECTION... In training the horse and rider should develop a greater level of connection. The rider has the feeling of the horse's hind quarters being elastically connected to the forehand and of the horse becoming more responsive to subtle changes in her position.

BEND AND STRAIGHTNESS... Bend and straightness are developed. The aim is to assist the horse to become supple and capable of bending equally well on both reins. Initially the rider's focus is on guiding the horse in a straight path. When travelling straight the footfalls of the hindquarters should land approximately where the front feet had previously been placed, both on straight lines and circles. Travelling straight is a precursor to 'straightness' which is a more advanced training goal.

THE SEAT

> "The seat should be thought of as an information centre, both a command centre and an area where the rider receives feedback from the horse." Robert Hall

The rider's seat is alpha and omega, both the beginning of the equestrian journey and the end. The seat is the main interface between human and horse; it is the rider's weightbearing area. As the horse is very sensitive to weight, when consideration is given to the combined weight of the saddle and the rider it is logical to assume that the horse will be most attentive to the subtle changes in the distribution of weight as he is responsible for balancing and counterbalancing it. It is therefore logical to predict that he will be more attentive to the influences of the seat than those of the legs and hands. The rider seeking a finessed system of communication with the horse is wise to consider which aids and influences a horse will be most attentive to.

THE DEVELOPMENT OF THE SEAT

The rider's seat develops in three main stages:

THE PASSIVE SEAT… The first seat a rider learns is to passively follow the horse's movements in all gaits without hindering or blocking them. The rider's hips are required to be flexible and supple to permit her seat to follow the three-dimensional movements of the horse's back. The pelvis and hips should move fluidly backwards and forwards, lowering and rising in unison with the horse's back. This may take many hours of practice to master.

THE DEEP SEAT… With more practice the rider develops a deeper, more elegant seat and rather than following the movements of the horse is now able to move in synchrony and harmony. A deep seat describes a seat with a lower centre of gravity that remains in close contact with the saddle at all times and as a consequence of this the rider can learn to influence the horse via her seat. The deep seat should not be confused with a heavy seat, which is that of a rider lacking self-carriage.

THE INDEPENDENT SEAT… The independent seat (or the educated seat) is a further development of the deep seat. The rider is capable of subtle influencing by isolating and using their seat and seatbones independently without inadvertently affecting other parts of their body. The use of subtle weight aids and of the seatbones to create bend, flexion and lateral movements have been mastered.

THE SEAT AND ITS EFFECT UPON THE HORSE'S BACK

It is important to recognise that a good seat cannot be developed without good support from the abdomen, lower back, and thighs. The thighs assist the seat in two ways, by spreading weight over a larger surface area and by helping support the stability of the upper body over the seat.

As the horse did not evolve for the purpose of carrying a rider, she is responsible for assisting the horse to develop the appropriate strength to support her. How heavily or lightly she sits will dramatically affect the movement through the horse's back and the activity of his legs.

The horse's back can be thought of as a bow and string. The 'string' is composed of the muscles and associated structures on the underside of the spine, the 'bow' is those located above the spine. The BOW is kept under tension by the STRING. If a rider sits heavily or if she restricts the flow of movement through the horse, the horse will not develop the correct musculature and the 'string' will be weak. The horse should carry the rider with his back bridged (a bow). He must step under his body with his hind legs to make a bridge of his back. If a rider sits heavily the bridge cannot be built.

RIDER TIP...

In an effort to deepen the seat do not bear downwards or press the seat into the saddle.

THE SEATBONES

The seatbones (or ischia) are surprisingly small in relation to their significance for guiding and aiding the horse. The seatbones are situated at the lowermost part of the pelvis and are rounded at the base. The lower back and abdomen can reposition the pelvis, and in consequence control which part of the rounded area of the seatbones are weightbearing.

THE CORRECT PELVIC POSITION

Riders aim to sit with their pelvis held level, neither tilted forwards nor backwards; this positions their weight over the middle area of the seatbones, and is termed the neutral position. In this position, the lumber spine should have a small curve which assists in absorbing the powerful forces that the horse generates.

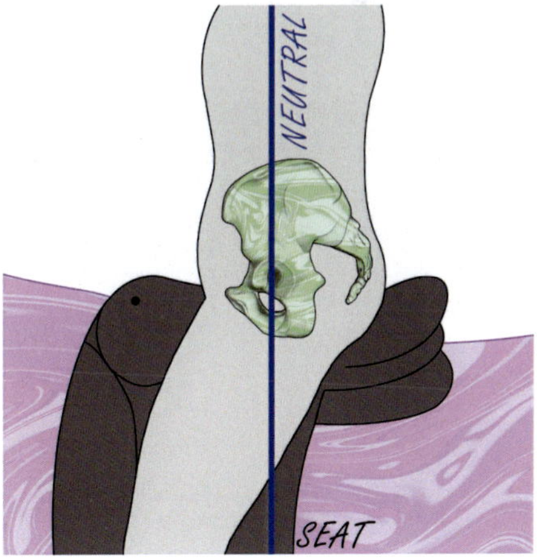

Although the rider's pelvis is in a constant state of motion when the horse is moving, it is wise after mounting to position the pelvis in neutral as this will best assist in synchronising movement with the horse. Some riders naturally align their pelvis to the neutral position; however, other riders must adjust their natural tilt to varying extents either backwards or forwards.

RIDER TIP...

By placing a hand under a seatbone and moving the upper body backwards and forwards, one can easily feel the changes in the weightbearing area of the seatbones.

RIDER TIP...

An excellent way to help maintain neutral pelvic alignment is to imagine the pelvis is filled with liquid, the aim being to avoid the liquid spilling out on to the horse.

INCORRECT PELVIC POSITIONS

There are, however, incorrect ways of sitting on a horse which should be understood in order that they might be avoided, namely the fork seat and the chair seat.

THE FORK SEAT... describes a riding position in which the upper pelvis is tilted forwards, causing the rider to sit on the front portion of the seatbones and the pubic arch (the fork). This pelvic alignment will cause the rider to tip forwards. The upper body is not easily supported when tipping forward, further instability occurs and the rider's legs will travel behind the correct vertical alignment, causing her to grip to retain balance. If her legs are resting too far back on the horse's side, they are incorrectly positioned for generating forward energy.

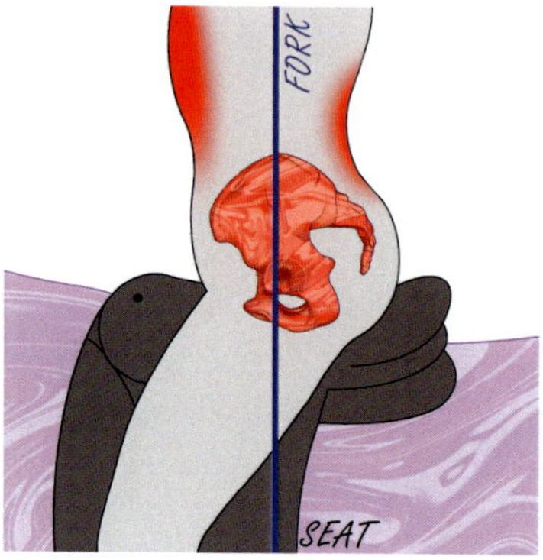

A slight lumber curve assists with the absorption of the horse's energetic movements. When aligned in the fork seat, the rider who wishes to correct the feeling of tipping may compensate by exaggerating her lumbar curve. An excessive lumbar curve cannot easily absorb the horse's movements and she may suffer lower back discomfort. If she further compensates by thrusting her chest out and shoulders backwards this will create unnatural tension in the upper back and shoulders and will affect the quality of the contact.

The fork seat blocks the horse's forward movement; however, adjusting to the neutral pelvic position often results in the horse moving freely forwards.

RIDER TIP...

If the pelvic tilt is not in the neutral position, to retain balance you will have to compensate throughout the rest of your body. Any other positional corrections you make will not result in an effective riding position.

THE CHAIR SEAT... (also known as the old hunting seat and the driving seat) describes a riding position in which the upper part of the pelvis is tilted backwards, causing the rider to sit on the back portion of her seatbones. This gives the impression that the rider is tucking her tailbone under. In this position, the rider's lumbar spine straightens. The loss of the lumbar curve affects the ability to absorb the horse's movement and can result in lower back pain.

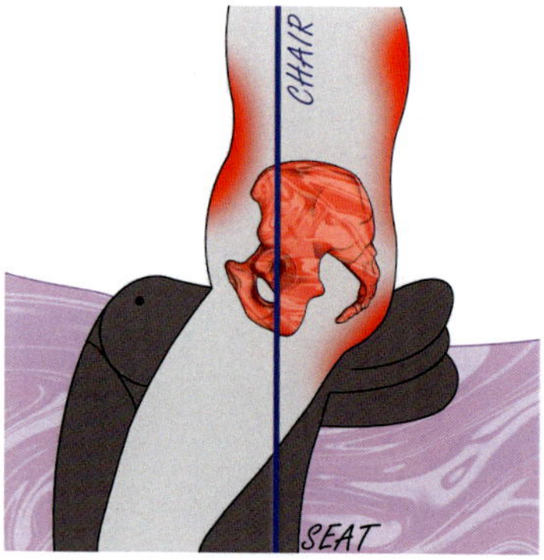

The chair seat pushes the rider's legs in front of the correct alignment, rendering them less effective. To retain balance, her chest collapses in on itself which adversely impacts the ability to breathe deeply.

A rider sitting on the back of her seatbones is inadvertently and constantly applying a driving aid. The lack of a cessation of the driving aid will result in the horse becoming unresponsive to these aids.

A rider positioned on the back of the seatbones concentrates her weight over a much smaller area of the seat and as a result puts pressure on a localised area of the horse's back, causing discomfort and preventing normal back function.

THE 2-POINT OR 3-POINT SEAT DEBATE AND THE DIFFERENCES BETWEEN THE MALE AND FEMALE PELVIC STRUCTURES

In the equestrian world a debate exists as to whether a rider's seat can be described as 2-point (the 2 seatbones) or 3-point (the 2 seatbones with additional support from the pubic arch). The answer to this conundrum most likely lies in a review of the anatomical differences between the male and female pelvises.

The seatbones of males and females are positioned and shaped differently. The female pelvis is wider and has a larger aperture to permit childbirth. This results in the female seatbones being set further apart than the males.

The female seatbones are shaped and angled differently from the males, they are narrower towards the pubic arch and widen significantly towards the posterior surface (towards the buttocks). The male's seatbones as a consequence of their narrower pelvis are positioned nearer to a parallel alignment.

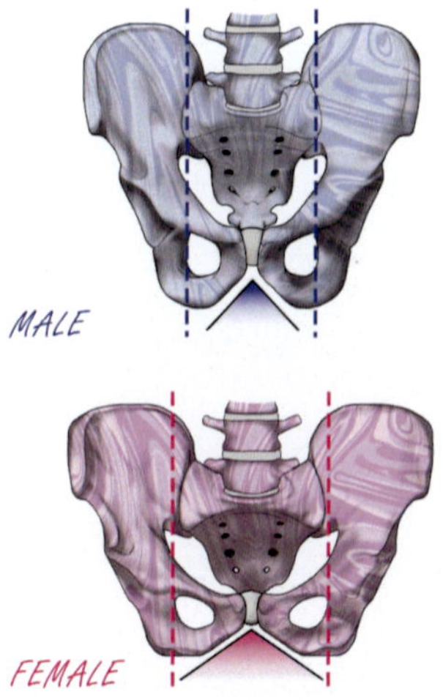

THE FEMALE SEATBONES ARE SET FURTHER APART THAN THE MALE

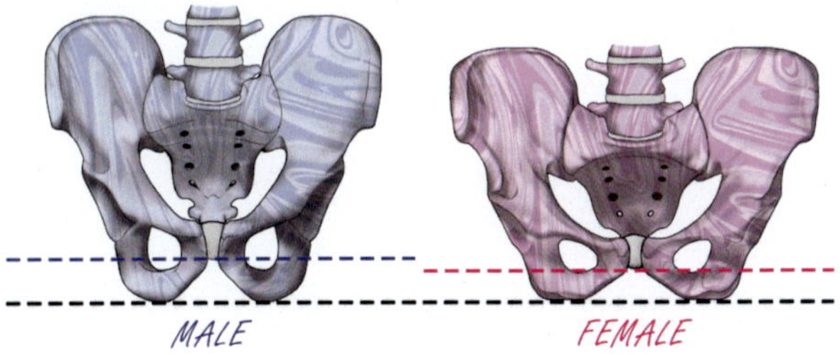

THE FEMALE PELVIC ARCH IS LOWER THAN THE MALE

Another significant gender related difference is the angle of the pubic arch; that of the male pelvis is narrower and higher than the female, whose pelvic arch is lower and wider.

CONCLUSIONS

In general, the surface area of the male seat is smaller than that of the female.

The pubic arch (the suggested 3rd point of contact or additional support) of males is usually narrower and higher than that of females. This would require male riders to tilt their pelvis significantly towards the fork seat if they wished to be in 3-point contact.

Saddle design and balance must play an influential role in the rider's experience of how their seat contacts the saddle. How much or how little each rider relies on their pubic arch for any support depends on the height of their pubic arch, their pelvic tilt, and the balance of the saddle.

It has been suggested that the male rides with a 2-point seat and the female with a 3-point seat. This is too simplistic a suggestion as there will be significant individual variation in pelvic structures.

FINAL THOUGHT... It could be suggested that some ride in a 3-point seat until they have refined their balance to a level that they do not require the occasional support of the pelvic arch. If riding in the 3-point seat, the vast majority of the rider's influence should be via the seatbones; the 3rd point should be subsidiary.

THE BASIC INFLUENCES OF THE SEAT

> "Sit up on the horse not down on it as though sitting on a chair. The seat must allow and encourage the horse to lift his back and step well underneath himself." Robert Hall

For riders wishing to ride with finesse, the use of the seat to influence the horse is a skill which can be refined. The aim is for the majority of the aids to be delivered via the seat, with the hands and legs used sparingly. If the rider's seat does not develop in its functionality, the rider will not be able to make significant progress.

Undoubtedly many actions of the seat must occur simultaneously or in sequence; to comprehend their influences each action should be considered alone.

ALLOWING WITH THE SEAT... the first role of the seat is that it should do no wrong, that it should be capable of inaction to allow the horse to move in his own rhythm by offering no restriction. The seat must permit the horse to move. The seat should not only be the rider's command centre, it should also be capable of inaction to receive feedback information from the horse.

THE LIGHTENED SEAT... is the least well understood use of the seat. The rider should stretch the upper body skywards without losing any contact with the saddle whilst lifting her pelvic floor. The aim is to indicate to the horse that you wish him to lift his back. This request can be supported by the action of the calves stretching down and lightly squeezing under the ribcage to ask the horse to lift his abdomen and back. A rider unfamiliar with using their seat in this fashion should imagine lifting the weight of her lower internal structures up into the lower rib cage.

The lightened seat should not be confused with the "half seat". When adopting the half seat, the rider lifts her seat bones off the saddle and places her weight in her stirrups. This seat is adopted by cross-country riders as it assists them to remain in dynamic balance at speed. Lifting the seat off the saddle is thought to encourage horses to lift and use their backs. The half seat in my opinion will not assist progress in flatwork training, where the aim is to encourage the forehand to lighten and the haunches to carry more weight. The half seat can place more weight on the front of the saddle, causing more weight to be carried by the horse's forehand.

THE RESTRICTING SEAT... is used for slowing down and stopping. It is used in the execution of the halt, half-halts, and in balanced transitions to slower paces. It involves the combined use of the lower back and abdomen to contain or filter the flow of the horse's energy. The rider restricts the movement of the horse by closing her legs against him, pulling her stomach towards a supporting lower back, and tightening the front of the torso and thighs. This action is momentary in the case of the half-halt and of longer duration in the case of the halt. This action of the seat allows the rider to control the tempo from the middle of the horse rather than by using the reins.

The restricting seat should be combined with the use of the lightened seat as the halt, half-halt, and transitions to a slower pace require the horse to lift his back and step underneath himself.

FORWARD MOVEMENT... to encourage forward movement the rider uses her lower back and stomach muscles to position herself towards the back of the seatbones, momentarily pushing with them. This aid is used to move the horse forwards from halt. When used once or twice and correctly timed with the rhythm of the gait it will encourage the horse to lengthen his stride. This aid should be used judiciously. Very importantly, the rider should return her pelvis to neutral after each aid. This action of the seat is often used in conjunction with leg aids, the aim is that the seat predominates and ultimately the seat alone will action a response. Overactive use of this aid or its constant application will result in the horse hollowing and the disengagement of his hind quarters.

When riding a responsive horse which is in front of the leg, it need only be applied once. On the less responsive horse this action of the seat can be used more than once but is best used briefly, then ceased, to allow the horse time to respond to it.

THE HANDS AND THE CONTACT

Contact describes the connection between the rider's hands and the horse's mouth. The rider's hands and the quality of the contact are the second most important area of influence over the horse. The quality of the contact affects a great deal more than just the horse's head and neck position. The contact can either allow freedom to move or can constrain by force. Crucially it will affect the horse's willingness to work with the rider. It will also assist or hinder forwardness, straightness, engagement, and his ability to balance, bend, collect and extend.

Instant communication with the horse is not possible without a consistent, elastic, and responsive connection. To obtain the best results, the rider wishing to ride in a refined way must be capable of instant interaction to enable the fine timing of their influences.

The hands, working in conjunction with the riding position, play an essential role in controlling the flow of the horse's energy.

HOW TO MAKE A GOOD CONTACT

> "Allow with the hands." Robert Hall

There are two equally important aspects in achieving a finessed contact. The first is the willingness of the horse to work forwards into the bit. The second is the quality and responsiveness of the rider's hands. If the horse is not sufficiently trusting of the rider's hands, she will be unable to achieve a good contact.

A good contact has its origins in tension-free, fluid movements. The rider should be relaxed with her contact, moving with the horse. The correct riding position is crucial in this, as is her balance, with the correct position, and good balance the quality of the contact will be subtle. The reins should never be used to assist balance.

Relaxed shoulders, tension free upper arms, and elbows will assist the responsiveness of the hands. Relaxed wrists will assist the movement of the hands forwards and help to minimise tension in the hands, allowing an unrestricted soft connection to the horse.

It is undoubtedly a skill to maintain a constant elastic connection. These tips may help:

- IT IS EASIER TO MAINTAIN AN ELASTIC CONTACT IF YOU CAN IMAGINE THAT YOUR HANDS BELONG TO THE HORSE'S MOUTH RATHER THAN TO YOUR BODY.
- THE HANDS MUST ALLOW THE HORSE TO STRETCH - THIS ASSISTS IN BUILDING THE CORRECT STRENGTH AND FLEXIBILITY FOR SELF-CARRIAGE.
- NEVER PULL BACKWARDS WITH THE HANDS.
- NEVER COMPRESS THE HORSE'S NECK.
- AVOID HAVING AN ON-OFF CONTACT OR LOOSE CONTACT.

RIDER TIP...

The contact you experience may vary as it can be affected by the horse's reactivity, energy and tension levels.

HOW A GOOD CONTACT FEELS

The hand should feel gently closed around the reins. It has been suggested that the feeling is similar to holding a small animal without letting it fall or hurting it.

A correct contact should feel equally soft and elastic in both hands. The contact should feel light, never being so heavy as to cause discomfort, pain or strain to the rider.

Importantly, the rider should always be able to feel the horse's head and neck moving up and down rhythmically within the stride. This movement can be felt twice per stride in both walk and trot and once per stride in canter.

THE RIDER'S HANDS AND THE WEIGHT THEY SHOULD SUPPORT

The perfect contact is only achievable when the horse has been trained to move in balance and self-carriage, no longer requiring support from the rider's hands. It feels equally light in both hands throughout.

The horse naturally uses his head and neck to assist his balance. He can stretch out his neck and lift or lower his head. During transitions, turns, acceleration and deceleration, his balance, weight distribution and centre of gravity is constantly altering. As a result, the weight in the rider's hands can change from moment to moment. In training, one of the aims is to improve the horse's balance, enabling him to become less reliant on the head and neck balancing mechanism.

When riding a well-balanced, well-trained horse there should be very little weight in the rider's hands.

RIDER TIP...

If the horse feels heavy in the hands, the rider should include more frequent half-halts and transitions to encourage the horse to lighten his forehand.

RIDER TIP...

A horse can only learn to lean on the hands if the rider permits it. If the horse is tired, let him rest; do not let him lean.

HOW TO HOLD THE REINS

When riding with a single rein, the rein should be placed snugly against the skin between the little finger and the ring finger. The hands close into soft fists with the thumbs uppermost. The hands should be held level, the distance between them roughly equal to the size of the horse's bit (i.e. between 5 to 6 inches apart). The thumbs held lightly closed over the forefingers should maintain a light pressure to prevent slippage of the rein.

The back of the hand should form a smooth continuous line to the forearm, the line from the elbow to horse's mouth being a straight line, unbroken at the wrist.

RIDER TIP...

The hands should never be tightly clenched as this tension is transmitted to the horse.

RIDER TIP...

A rider with small hands will find it easier to use thinner reins. If riding using thick reins, she cannot achieve a sensitive contact if she struggles to close, release and vary the pressure on the reins.

RIDER TIP...

Gloves can be very useful to help prevent rein slippage.

HOW TO HOLD TWO REINS

In a double bridle there are two bits, each with a rein attached. The bradoon sits uppermost in the horse's mouth above the weymouth. It requires considerable skill and refined finger control to operate the reins of the double bridle independently.

The actions of the bits and bridle apply pressure to various parts of the horse's head: the tongue, the corners of the lips, the curb groove, the poll, and the roof of the mouth. Many horses are understandably sensitive to such pressures, particularly pressure on the poll, curb groove and the roof of the mouth.

Traditionally, in the UK the reins attached to the left side of the bradoon and weymouth are held in the left hand, the reins attached to the right side of the bradoon and weymouth in the right hand. The variations of this option are crossed and uncrossed. When crossed, the weymouth rein is held between the ring and the middle fingers and the bradoon rein between the little and ring fingers.

When uncrossed, the bradoon rein is held between the ring and the middle fingers, while the weymouth rein is held between the little and ring fingers.

RIDER TIP...

Do not expect the horse to work on the same rein length for the whole of a training session. Always reward a horse for good efforts with breaks on a long rein for stretching.

REIN LENGTH

Finding the optimum rein length for the horse can prove difficult. If the reins are too short, the arms are stretched excessively in front of the trunk, affecting the rider's stability. If too long or looping, the rider will not have the instant control which is necessary for subtle aiding. Additionally, the length of the reins directly influences the position of the horse's head and neck and affects the freedom of movement.

Finally, it is to be noted that the rein length is not necessarily constant and should be monitored and adjusted throughout the training session. The rider should be responsive to changes in the horse's frame and to variations in the horse's head position throughout the session.

SHOULD THE HANDS BE CARRIED HIGH OR LOW?

The height at which the hands are carried is largely determined by the horse's conformation.

The horse's neck set will affect hand height, a neck which is set lower into the chest requiring the hands to be carried lower.

CONTACT ISSUES

> "The bit is only as harsh as the hands operating it." Author Unknown

Horses can evade the contact in different ways and for different reasons. Getting to the root cause of evasions may take time and is often a process of elimination.

Incorrect bitting can create many issues. For clear communication, bits must be of the correct size and be adjusted to the optimal height. If fitted too high in the mouth, they apply constant pressure, rendering the rider incapable of subtle connection. Conversely, if the bit is fitted too low, communication will be inconsistent and, like a faulty phone connection, essential parts of the conversation will be missed.

RIDER TIP...

It is wise to be familiar with the effects of the bit before riding. Different bits have differing intended actions and the areas where they can apply pressure vary.

RIDER TIP...

Over time, as bridles are used and cleaned, the leather will stretch; make time to check the fit of the bit regularly.

THE HORSE'S HEAD POSITION AND A PHYSIOLOGICAL EXPLANATION OF CONTACT

Currently too much emphasis is placed upon the horse's head position in training and in competition. The intelligent rider should wish to understand the far-reaching effects of the quality of the contact on the movement of the horse, rather than simply its effects on the head and neck position.

THE HORSE'S HEAD POSITION

The horse's head position is often discussed with reference to "the vertical". When viewing the horse's head from the side, the vertical is the imaginary vertical line which can be drawn from the horse's forehead towards the ground. The ridden horse's nose can be observed to be behind, on or in front of this line.

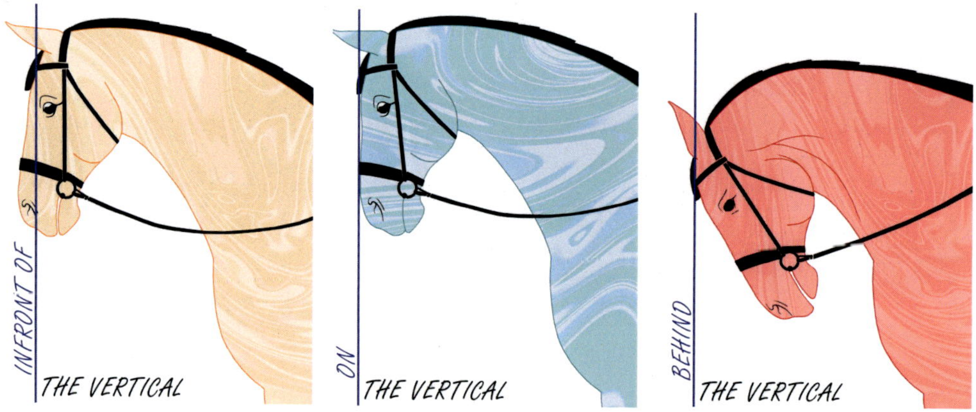

ON THE VERTICAL (OTV)... describes the horse's head position when a straight vertical line can be drawn from browband to the ground.

IN FRONT OF THE VERTICAL (IFV)... describes the horse's head position when the nose is carried ahead of the browband.

BEHIND THE VERTICAL (BTV)... describes a horse's head position when the nose is carried near to his chest, behind the browband.

In nature the horse uses his head and neck for balance. When travelling at speed, the head is normally observed to be in front of the vertical as this position functions best for both his balance and vision. Regarding his vision, the equine retina has two areas of acute perception: a high-acuity spot, called the area centralis and the visual streak which extends in a horizontal band across the retina which allows the horse to scan the horizon.

Horses in the early stages of training carry their head and neck lower, moving with their heads in front of the vertical. It is only when the horse is trained correctly and working in collected paces that his face will naturally move towards the vertical, thus the ridden horse's head position reflects his level of training.

Decades ago it was a rare occurrence to see young partially trained horses being ridden on the vertical or behind the vertical. Today it is becoming increasingly more common. Horses that are pulled into a shortened head and neck position struggle to track-up and cannot move correctly through their back and shoulders. Restraining the head creates a chain reaction of dysfunction.

No ethical riding system should ever endorse the positioning of the horse's head behind the vertical. Excessive bit pressure can cause horses to carry their heads behind the vertical in an attempt to escape the discomfort. Scientific studies have shown that when the horse's head is positioned behind the vertical his breathing is constricted, his vision is impaired and structures within the neck and gullet may be damaged. It is believed that the horse suffers psychological stress as a result of being physically compromised.

THE POSITION OF THE HORSE'S HEAD AND NECK SHOULD BE ALLOWED TO DEVELOP OVER TIME AND BE THE RESULT OF CORRECT TRAINING METHODS.

THE BIT AND ITS INFLUENCES

The bit is a control device, that is largely accepted as the means to assist in the control of direction and movement. Subtle pressure applied to a bit and its timed release effects trained responses. The first response the horse learns is to stop when pressure is applied to the bit.

The mouthpiece of a bit lies over the horse's tongue and the bars of the mouth (an area of his mouth between the incisors and the molars). If bitted with a simple snaffle, when pressure is applied this will mainly be felt on his tongue, the corners of his mouth and to a lesser extent the bars of the mouth. All three of these areas are understandably very sensitive to damage and pressure. In particular the horse's tongue is very sensitive, the edges of the tongue being more sensitive than the middle. It is easily damaged and contains many receptors which react to pressure, pain and temperature. Comprised of more than a dozen muscles, the tongue has a highly mobile forward section which works together with the teeth and lips to select and pick up food. The back of the tongue is used to assist in chewing and swallowing. It is covered with taste buds which may explain why some horses may dislike the taste of certain metals or bit surfaces.

The bit's actions are part of the accepted communication system with the horse. The rider should therefore consider the sensitivity of her hands and the connection they make with the horse's mouth. Crucially she can refine these movements if she wishes to communicate with the horse via subtle influences. Understanding certain aspects of the horse's physiology can make it possible to gain greater insight into the influence of bit pressure on the horse's movement. The two important areas to consider are the poll and the hyoid apparatus. A rider who comprehends these influences will as a consequence use her hands with more empathy. There is no evidence to suggest that the horse's mouth is any less sensitive than that of any other mammal.

THE HYOID APPARATUS

A PHYSICAL CONNECTION EXISTS BETWEEN THE HORSE'S HIND FEET, THROUGH HIS BODY TO HIS MOUTH.

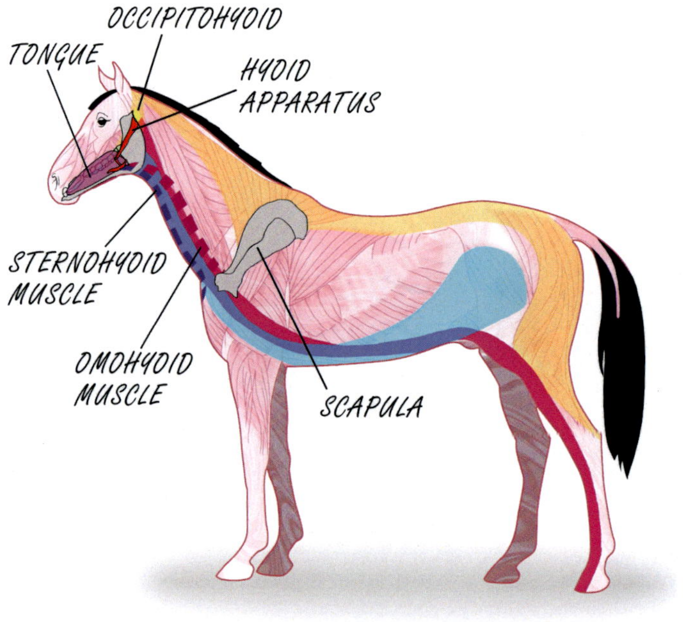

The horse's hyoid apparatus is an important structure with far-reaching connections from his nose to his tail. It is now accepted that excessive bit pressure affects the hyoid apparatus and as a result negatively impacts the function and mobility of both the horse's front and hind legs.

The hyoid apparatus is the collective term for the bones which suspend the tongue and larynx. It consists of pairs of bones, and a single basihyoid bone. The hyoid apparatus is situated under the lower jawbone and in front of the upper spine. It has direct attachments to the horse's tongue, the larynx, and the cervical spine. The hyoid bones are also connected to a group of muscles extending down to the sternum, shoulders, and forelegs. These muscles extend yet further in the horse's body to the breast, pectoral and abdominal muscles and connect to the pelvis.

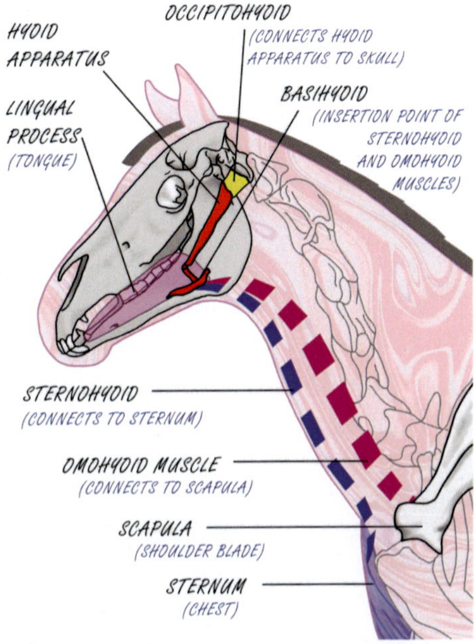

There exists a physical connection from the horse's hind feet to his mouth via muscles and fasciae. The fasciae are connective tissues that lie under the skin in large sheets. They weave around muscles connecting muscles to the structures associated with motion. They form a continuous link through the horse's body from the hyoid apparatus via the trunk to the pelvis and hind limbs.

This is important to consider as most bits function by the use of tongue pressure; pressure on the tongue can influence the freedom of movement throughout the horse's entire body. Any restrictions in the functioning of any of these structures will negatively impact the movement of the horse.

Crucially for riders the hyoid apparatus influences the horse's poll area and as a consequence relaxation and flexion in that area.

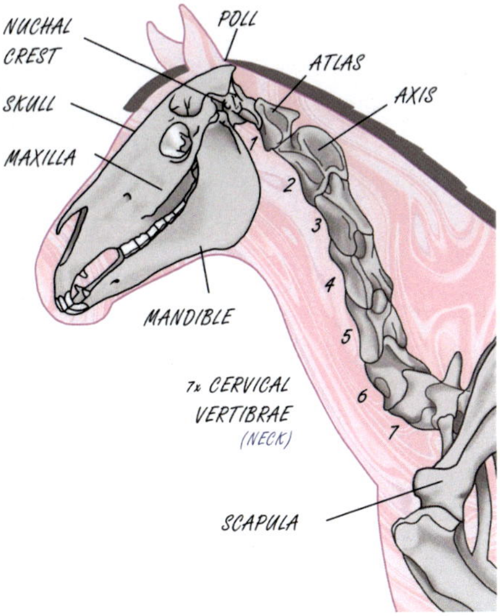

THE POLL

The poll area, as a consequence of its connections to other muscle groups, plays a very important role in the fluidity of the horse's movement. The poll is a protrusion at the highest point of the equine skull. Many important tendons and muscles attach at the poll. Due to the pressure that can be applied by the bridle headpiece and the upper portion of the headcollar it is an area which is vulnerable to damage. The horse's energy and movement flows from the back feet through the body, neck and ultimately into the rider's hand. Injury, tension, or restriction at the poll will break this elastic connection.

The tongue, the hyoid apparatus and the poll are sensitively interconnected. Tension in one area will impact upon another and importantly relaxation in one area can release tension in its counterparts. The relaxation of the tongue and jaws through their physical connection to the hyoid apparatus can influence relaxation and flexion at the poll. Consequently it is important that the horse's jaws be able to move freely to facilitate true relaxation of the poll. The horse's jaws should not be restricted by tight nosebands or flash noseband attachments.

When equestrians talk of relaxation at the poll or flexion of the poll, they are in fact referring to the area behind the poll, the first two vertebrae of the neck which form a curved ridge at the top of the neck.

Relaxation at the poll is dependent on the horse's ability to stretch the top area of his neck, the area where C1 (the atlas) and C2 (the axis) are located. The atlas connects to the axis in such a way that the horse is capable of nodding his head up and down without moving the rest of his body. This enables him to decrease or increase the angle of the head relative to his neck.

FLEXING AND RELAXATION OF THE POLL: HOW TO ENCOURAGE IT

The correct rein contact is associated with relaxed wrists, elbows and shoulders, the rider's lack of tension encourages the horse to stretch forward and connect his back legs through his body to his mouth, encouraging correct athletic development.

Riding with light responsive hands should encourage the horse to place trust in the gentleness and sensitivity of the rider's hands; this in turn should result in his mental and physical relaxation. This physical and mental release of tension permits the horse to release tension in the muscles around the poll, allowing the horse's head to flex longitudinally, dropping towards vertical alignment.

Relaxation at the poll is best achieved by riding with a light, giving contact, responsive to the horse's desire to stretch. The horse should be allowed to stretch forward and release unnecessary tension at the top of his neck in the C1 and C2 area. It is essential that his jowl angle is not reduced as this may partially obstruct the upper airways. The rider should have the feeling of the horse's neck lifting upwards and outwards from the chest, stretching forwards and around into the contact as this opens the jowl angle. Any backwards pull on the reins will reduce the jowl angle and will affect the horse's willingness to relax and flex into the contact.

Relaxation at the poll can be felt by the rider's hands, as can the opposite feeling, of tension when a horse lifts his head up against the contact. The horse should be encouraged to relax and flex the poll longitudinally.

As the rider's hands and contact can play a vital role in the relaxation of the horse's tongue and jaw, the horse should be encouraged to relax the jaw and tongue by very gentle vibrations of the rein. Small vibrations are often more effective than large vibrations. It is wise to start with the tiniest possible movement and build up to a level that results in the release of tension. Horses will vary in their preference for different rhythms of vibrations and their frequency. When aiding, the aim is always to use the smallest possible aid. Importantly, avoid vibrating the reins in alternative movements as this may train the horse to move his nose from side to side.

RIDER TIP...

Tension at the poll can be caused by poor contact, incorrect bitting, excessive bridle pressure or noseband pressure. It may also indicate general discomfort or pain.

RIDER TIP...

It is important for riders to relax their own jaw, neck, shoulders, and elbows in order to have a constant elastic connection with the horse's mouth.

THE RIDING POSITION IN DETAIL

> "Do you want to do this the easy way or the hard way?"
> John Haddow, my father.

Why place so much importance on the riding position? There are two ways of learning: one option is to acquaint yourself with the appropriate information; the other is trial and error. As a young child my father taught me an important life lesson. When he was carrying out home improvements I was keen to 'help' him. My natural inclination was always to rush in and get started, then relatively quickly I would become disinterested because I was disappointed with my poor results. Before each task, my father started asking me if I wanted to do the job the easy way or the hard way. I would always respond with 'the easy way', grab tools, and start off with no plan. Eventually I realised that what I believed to be the easy way was in fact the hard way. The easiest and quickest way to perform well is to acquaint yourself with the appropriate information before carrying out a task.

THE BENEFITS OF A GOOD RIDING POSITION

- PERMITS THE HORSE TO MOVE FREELY WITHOUT ANY UNINTENTIONAL RESTRICTION OF MOVEMENT
- DISTRIBUTES THE RIDER'S WEIGHT EVENLY OVER THE SEAT ENABLING THE HORSE TO CARRY HER MORE EASILY IN BALANCE
- ENABLES THE RIDER TO STAY IN DYNAMIC BALANCE, ESPECIALLY WHEN THE HORSE ACCELERATES AND DECELERATES
- HELPS THE RIDER TO DEVELOP A DEEPER, MORE INDEPENDENT SEAT
- ALLOWS THE RIDER TO MOVE HARMONIOUSLY WITH THE HORSE
- ENABLES THE RIDER TO BE STABLE IN MOTION AND ELIMINATES UNNECESSARY RIDER MOVEMENTS
- GREATER POSITIONAL STABILITY ENABLES PRECISE AIDING, CLARITY OF COMMUNICATION, ENABLING THE RIDER TO USE SENSITIVE AND SUBTLE AIDS

THE RIDING POSITION IS AN INSTRUMENT WHICH CAN BE FINE-TUNED TO HARMONISE WITH THE HORSE OR IT CAN BE USED AS A BLUNT TOOL TO APPLY PRESSURE UNTIL SOMETHING GIVES.

To become elegant, the rider's movements should be the equal of her mount. They should be equally fluid and balanced with the appearance of effortlessness. The riding position must appear to be still; much is going on below the surface which is not visible, nonetheless the horse can detect it. The rider who wishes to put thought into the improvement and fine-tuning of her riding position will find this is the quickest route to improvement.

IMPORTANTLY THE RIDING POSITION SHOULD BE FREE OF STIFFNESS AND IT SHOULD NOT ADVERSELY IMPACT UPON THE HORSE'S MOVEMENT

The rider should sit upon the horse, supporting her upper body, not slouching, nor collapsing at the waist. Maintaining the correct body alignment will not only assist balance but will help the rider in absorbing the bouncing action of the trot and the bounding action of canter.

EAR, SHOULDER, HIPBONE AND HEEL SHOULD BE IN VERTICAL ALIGNMENT

To encourage the horse to develop self-carriage, the rider should work to improve their posture when mounted and unmounted. If she wishes her horse to be in self-carriage she must be capable of self-carriage.

THE RIDER'S LOWER BODY

THE ABDOMEN, LOWER BACK AND THEIR IMPORTANCE

The importance and use of the rider's lower back and abdomen is all too often omitted when discussing the function of the riding position and the aids.

The lower back and abdomen influence the rider's seat, her pelvic tilt, and the action of her seatbones. They play a crucial role in maintaining the correct pelvis tilt in motion.

They are also an essential cog in the mechanism which allows the flow of the horse's free forward movement and in the containment of it.

To assist in maintaining the correct position the lumber region should have a small natural curve. The rider's lumber area should be both strong and flexible. It must be strong enough to be capable of advancing each hip independently to aid the horse and to facilitate precision aiding.

The stomach should be sufficiently relaxed to allow the horse's movement to flow. When transitioning to a slower gait, the stomach should be drawn towards a supporting lower back to assist with balanced deceleration. Overtightening of the stomach can tilt the pelvis, positioning the rider on to the back of the seatbones into the undesirable driving seat.

The rider's lumbar area should be free of stiffness, able to move supplely and freely in all directions with the movement of the horse's pelvis. The abdomen should not be pulled in tightly but should function in conjunction with the back muscles and thighs to stabilise the upper body.

The buttocks must be relaxed, permitting the seatbones to make close contact with the saddle.

RIDER TIP...

It can help to imagine the horse's energy flowing in through the lower back and out through the stomach and hands. Aim to control this energy with postural tension in preference to using the hands.

THE LEG POSITION

The correct non-aiding leg position has its origins in a supple pelvic area. When aiding, the legs must move to influence different areas of the horse's sides: on the girth, behind the girth and in front of the girth. These leg positions are only feasible if the rider has sufficiently flexible hips and relaxed buttocks.

The thighs as the largest muscles in the human body are a useful part of the body's mechanism for absorbing the energy of the horse. They assist in spreading the rider's weight over a larger area and are crucial in assisting the rider to develop a deep and independent seat. The thighs should be turned into and onto the saddle from the hips, until they rest flat against the saddle.

The hip joint and heel should be in vertical alignment, the thighs and knees rotated inwards until the toes point forwards, the length of the rider's foot parallel to the horse's side. This positions the inside of the calf muscles against the horse, enabling them to be used to aid. With the calves in the correct position, they can work in unison with the leg adductor and abductor muscles, to apply subtle aids.

If a rider's knees and toes point outwards, she will find it harder to use the calves for aiding and may need to use her heels. Crucially, she will find it difficult to achieve true longitudinal bend as she is unable to coordinate the use of the inside seatbone, inner thigh and inner calf to facilitate bend.

RIDER TIP...

If the thighs are tensed, they cannot assist in energy absorption and will negatively affect seat security.

The weight of the rider's legs should drop naturally into the heels. They should hang long and comfortably, permitting influence over the lower part of the horse's torso; applying the leg under the horse's ribcage can assist the horse to lift its back.

The legs should not grip on to the horse's sides nor restrict the natural breathing movements of the horse's ribcage. The rider should be able to feel the horse's sides expand and contract when he breathes. Gripping legs can cause the horse to carry itself stiffly, restricting the horse's ability to bend longitudinally.

Softly bent knees, relaxed ankles, and relaxed feet will allow the heels to lower.

RIDER TIP...

Gripping with the knees, legs or calves will cause the legs to shorten and the heels to rise.

HOW MUCH OF THE CALF SHOULD BE IN CONTACT WITH THE HORSE'S SIDE?

How much of the calf is in contact with the horse is dependent on the rider's height and the shape of the horse's ribcage. A short rider on a large horse will have most of her calf and possibly the inside of her foot in contact with the horse. A tall rider will have most of her calf hanging past the widest part of the horse's ribcage. The perfect position is when the inside part of the upper calf muscle is in light contact with the horse's side.

THE FEET, ANKLES, HEELS AND TOES

RIDER TIP...

Imagining that the heels of the riding boots are made of heavy metal can assist the calves to release and the heels to lower.

The mobility of the ankle joints is key to foot and toe position. The ankles should be relaxed and supple.

Although, it is acceptable for the feet to lie horizontally, crucially the heels should not be forced down causing tightening in the calves. The heel ideally should be positioned slightly lower than the ball of the foot.

If the foot is not correctly placed in the stirrup iron this can result in toe curling or gripping. The toes should be relaxed and neither curling under nor gripping inside the boot.

PLACING THE FOOT CORRECTLY IN THE STIRRUP IRON

The correct placement of the foot in the stirrup iron greatly enhances the leg position and consequently assists rider balance. The broadest part of the foot (the ball of the foot) should be placed straight and centrally in the stirrup. An even weight distribution across the foot gives the best support and avoids uneven strain on the knees.

The stirrup irons should sit level, bearing sufficient weight to retain them in position. Placing too much of the foot through the stirrup will put pressure on the arch of the foot. If only the tips of the toes are placed through the stirrup, the toes will curl and grip.

RIDER TIP...

To check the position and stability of your legs, after riding examine the grease on the back of the boots. There should be no grease to the outside of the back seams. The grease thickness will also inform whether one leg was used preferentially.

THE RIDER'S UPPER BODY

> "The upper body from the waist remaining stable and level, the lower body absorbing much of the movement and moving with the horse."
> Robert Hall

The upper body's position and influence in placing sufficient weight on the seatbones is equally as important as the influences of the lower body. The upper body should be held in self-carriage without stiffness in a naturally erect posture. It should gently stretch upwards to full upper body height. The chest should be open, shoulders sitting level, and lightly placed back, correctly aligned with the ear, hip, and heel. The rider's body above the waist should largely remain in alignment, outwardly unaffected by the movement of her pelvis.

THE RIDER'S HEAD AND NECK

As an adult head weighs around 10-11lbs, its incorrect positioning can necessitate a chain reaction of postural compensations.

The head and neck should be comfortably aligned, gently stretched upwards and carried level, not tilted forwards, nor backwards, nor to the side. The neck should be softly stretched upwards to provide a secure support for the head. The chin should sit level and be gently tucked to assist the correct spinal alignment. The jaws should be relaxed, and the teeth should not be clenched. The rider's neck should be sufficiently supple to look directly over her shoulders.

A horse can discern changes in the rider's gaze and any turning of the shoulders. These movements can be felt by him as slight changes in the weight distribution of the seat; consequently the rider should look in the direction in which they are going. The rider should direct her gaze over the poll, rather than through the horse's ears. The rider's gaze should be horizontal. If she looks through the horse's ears this will encourage her to hang her head slightly forwards and will render the action of the seatbones less effective.

RIDER TIP...

To correct head tilt, focus on keeping your nose in line with your sternum or the front zipper of your jacket.

RIDER TIP...

Do not look too far ahead on turns and circles as this can cause the horse to fall in.

RIDER TIP...

Using peripheral vision to locate dressage markers and memorising the arena layout will help avoid unnecessary head movements. It is possible to look down with the eyes only whilst keeping the head in alignment.

THE WAIST

The rider's waist must be sufficiently supple to permit the upper body and shoulders to remain level and symmetrically placed over the horse at all times. When the horse lowers and lifts his back, the rider's waist should lengthen and shorten accordingly to permit the shoulders to remain level.

The waist should be sufficiently toned to prevent collapsing or tipping. When riding circles and voltes, the waist should swivel; the smaller the circle the more the waist should turn inwards.

RIDER TIP...

The rider should not look down when turning as this may cause the inside shoulder to drop and the waist to collapse.

THE RIDER'S BACK AND UPPER BODY

Tipping forwards should be avoided as it destabilises both horse and rider.

However, in rising trot a slight forward inclination of the upper body is acceptable as this may assist the rider to remain in dynamic balance. The main focus in rising trot should be minimising the rising action and landing lightly in the saddle.

RIDER TIP...

Care should be taken to avoid the upper body falling significantly in front of or behind the correct vertical alignment.

THE RIDER'S CHEST AND SHOULDERS

The rider's thoracic spine should stretch upwards from the waist, the chest should be open with the shoulders gently placed back, sitting horizontally level, positioned in vertical alignment with the ear, hip and heel. The chest should be expanded, the bottom ribs lifted. An incorrect shoulder position should not be remedied by forcing the shoulders back as this creates tension in the neck and negatively affects the rider's contact. To achieve relaxed and correctly aligned shoulders, the rider must engage the use of the erector spinae muscles (the back muscles that run down either side of the spinal column).

RIDER TIP...

Rounded shoulders can be corrected by lifting the lower ribs, thus repositioning the upper body.

RIDER TIP...

Tense shoulders can be helped by lifting the shoulders as high as possible and holding this position as long as possible. When the muscles tire, then release; the shoulders should drop into a better position. Repeating this exercise can help to develop body awareness of the shoulder positioning.

RIDER TIP...

Be careful of opening the chest too far, to a point where it is thrust forwards, causing the lumbar spine to over-curve to compensate.

THE IMPORTANCE OF BREATHING

The importance of breathing correctly when riding cannot be overstated. Riders when anxious or concentrating may hold the breath or take shallow breaths. Failure to breathe deeply prevents the natural breathing pattern; this reduces the distribution of oxygen around the body, causing fatigue.

THE RIDER'S ARMS

> "Elbow, hand and horse's mouth should form a straight line which should not be broken at the wrist." Robert Hall

The rider's arms should drop loosely from relaxed shoulders. The forearms should be slightly lifted to form a straight line through the hand, to the horse's mouth. A relaxed upper arm, elbow and lower arm allows the wrist and hand, when correctly positioned, to move freely forwards when required by the horse.

The elbows should sit slightly in advance of the vertical alignment of ear, shoulder, hip joint, and heel. The elbows should not be pinned to the sides nor should they stick outwards. The elbows should be free to move, responsive to changes in the horse's frame. The wrists should be flexible, relaxed, not turning inwards nor outwards, forming an unbroken connection to the horse's mouth.

RIDER TIP...

The elbows should not be carried behind nor travel behind the vertical rider alignment.

RIDER TIP...

Riding with the elbows positioned too far in front of the body can cause the arms to be unreactive and can adversely affect rider balance. Any pull will tip her forwards.

THE RIDER'S HANDS

An essential part of finessed riding skills is developing a good sensitive contact with the horse's mouth. The hands must become independent in order to develop feel.

The hands should form soft fists, the thumbs positioned uppermost, gently held over the reins to prevent rein slippage. The hands should not be clenched; excessive stiffness or tension in the fingers will cause discomfort to the horse. The snaffle rein should be held well tucked into the base between the little finger and ring finger.

The hands should be held level, the distance between them being roughly equal to the size of the horse's bit. This assists the rider to influence the corners of the mouth sensitively.

The hands should remain either side of the mane, never crossing over. The fingers should have dexterity capable of opening and closing independently of each other, communicating with the horse's mouth softly and subtly via finger tension alone.

RIDER TIP...

Imagining that the hands belong more to the horse than the rider will assist with the elastic feeling of connectivity.

RIDER CHECK ONCE MOUNTED...

THE EAR, SHOULDER, HIP AND HEEL SHOULD BE IN VERTICAL ALIGNMENT

- Place the seatbones in the deepest part of the saddle with the weight distributed equally over them. Relax the buttocks.
- Stretch the upper body vertically to full upper body height.
- Hold the head and chin level; direct the gaze over the horse's poll.
- Gently lift the lower ribcage, opening the chest. Hold the shoulders level, allowing them to drop into vertical alignment.
- The elbows, wrists and hands should connect to the bit in an unbroken line.
- Make a soft fist with the hands, the thumbs softly closed over the fingers. Hold the hands level, placed either side of the horse's neck.
- The seat, hips and pelvis should be flexible, moving in harmony with the horse.
- Relax the legs, lightly drape them around the horse, drop the weight of the legs into the heels and keep them free of any gripping action.
- Rotate the thighs and knees inwards until the toes are pointing forwards and the inside of the calves are lying on or slightly off the horse's side.

EQUINE MOVEMENT AND WALK, TROT AND CANTER

The rider should be familiar with the natural gaits of the horse – how they might be preserved, influenced and further enhanced.

> 'The horse knows how to move. The rider's job is to allow it to move.'
> Robert Hall

THE SCIENCE OF MOVEMENT: THE CENTRAL PATTERN GENERATORS

In all vertebrates, including horses, control over the rhythmic movements of the gaits lies in specialised nerve cells located throughout the lower thoracic and lumbar regions of the spinal cord, called central pattern generators. These specialised neural oscillators can be influenced by the brain but can also function independently, creating natural, unhurried and fluid rhythmical movement. The wise rider will be wary of interfering with this natural rhythm.

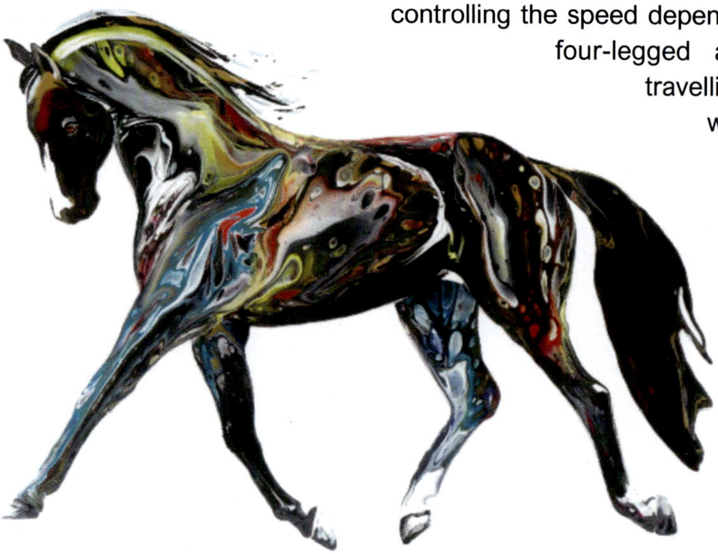

The central pattern generators are also responsible for controlling the speed dependent gait transitions in all four-legged animals. If a horse is travelling too quickly in trot they will trigger a transition into canter or if he is trotting too slowly they will trigger a transition into walk. At times, the horse will consciously decide to transition into a different gait without being asked. On other occasions the transitions will have been actioned by the central pattern generators.

A foal is born with the capability of moving rhythmically in all gaits. In place at birth is a neural connectedness which takes the form of diagonal pairing that occurs in trot and canter. This connectedness can be utilised by the rider to increase or decrease stride length. A longer or shorter stride in one leg of a diagonal pairing affects stride length in the associated paired leg. A longer stride in the left hind is associated with a longer stride in the right front leg. It is therefore possible to increase or shorten stride length by timing the aids to influence either the hind legs (the more traditional method) or the front legs, knowing that the diagonally associated legs will react accordingly.

THE GAIT CYCLE

As a prey animal, the horse has evolved over thousands of years to be an exceptional athlete. He has long limbs; the weight of his muscles is concentrated in the upper section of the limbs and around his hips and shoulders. His lower limbs are largely comprised of lightweight structures (tendons and bones) which enables them to be moved forwards easily. These biological adaptations have resulted in exceptional athleticism and also enable energy efficient movement.

Each of the four legs involved in a gait cycle works in different ways: moving (braking phase and thrusting phase); supporting the body (stance phase) and repositioning itself (the swing phase). The horse can adjust each of these phases to change the characteristics of his gaits.

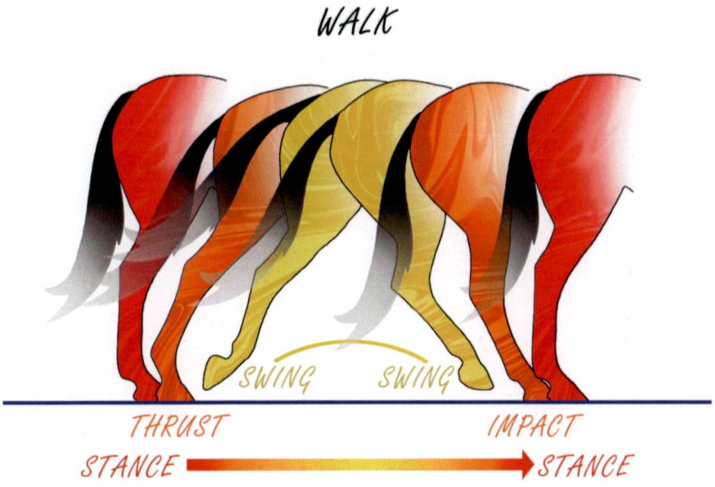

DRESSAGE TRAINING INVOLVES CHANGING THE BASIC PATTERNS OF BRAKING AND PROPULSION IN THE LIMBS

THE GROUND REACTION FORCES

The *Ground Reaction Force* (GRF) is the force which assists the horse to move. When the horse's hoof is on the ground, it must push against the ground to move, the GRF is the reaction of the ground pushing back against the hoof. The horse utilises the angles of the GRF to control his balance, speed, and direction. The ground reaction forces are of importance in understanding how the gaits can be influenced or improved.

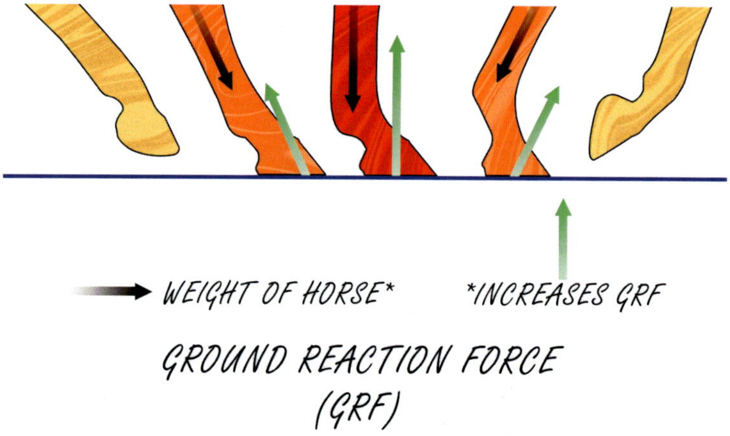

GAIT IMPROVEMENT

Each horse has a natural way of going in all gaits. This is to some extent defined by his conformation and muscular strength. When a horse walks, he has a more fluid gait if he can 'move at his own natural speed'. If he is hurrying to keep up with another horse who walks more quickly, his gait will become less fluid. When the rider hurries the horse, this pushes him out of balance and as a consequence causes him to travel on his forehand.

The aim when riding is to focus on natural rhythm, and to train the horse in such a way as to best improve him whilst preserving that which is inherently beautiful.

The horse's body in movement involves two sets of opposing forces: one set from the hind limb (often referred to as the engine of the horse) which propel the horse forwards, and the second set from the forelimbs which function by preventing the powerful force of the hind limbs from pushing the horse downwards on to the forehand. A crucial component of dynamic balance and self-carriage is the ability to use the braking activity of the front limbs to move the horse's centre of gravity towards his haunches.

GAIT ADJUSTMENTS

STRIDE LENGTH... The horse can lengthen or shorten the stride by adjusting the protraction and retraction of his limbs and the breaking and thrusting forces he applies to the ground.

DURATION OF THE SWING PHASE... The slower the horse moves the greater the stance phase and the greater the potential propulsion. By controlling the swing phase the horse influences the amount of propulsion he can apply.

STANCE PHASE... Increasing the stance phase can result in greater propulsion. In the half-halt, the rider should ask the horse to dwell briefly on a hind hoof to increase propulsion.

THE PLACEMENT OF THE HIND LIMBS... The hind limb should be placed well under the horse to assist propulsion. The more engaged the hindquarters and the more the horse propels himself forwards, the more likely this powerful force will rotate the horse on to his forehand. Therefore, to maintain correct balance, the forelimbs must work harder, using breaking forces to redirect his body upwards.

GREATER FLEXING OF THE JOINTS IN THE HIND LIMBS... When the angles of compressed joints are opened, the horse can produce significant amounts of propulsive force as evidenced when the horse jumps an obstacle.

TEMPO... The rate at which the rhythm of a gait is repeated is called the tempo. The horse can increase or decrease the tempo of a gait.

LATERAL MOVEMENT... The horse can move laterally in walk, trot and canter by changing the direction of the forces he applies to the ground and using this sideways push to assist his limbs in adducting and abducting.

THE GAITS: WALK, TROT AND CANTER...

THE WALK

The walk should have a four beat rhythm: four distinctive regular footfalls should be detectable. The walk has a predictable sequence: left hind, left foreleg, right hind, right foreleg. There is no moment of suspension in walk; two or three hooves are always on the ground, the horse's pelvis rotating, rising and dropping significantly.

The walk is the least expressive of the three basic gaits and as such its importance in training is often overlooked. The qualities of the walk are good indicators of correct training.

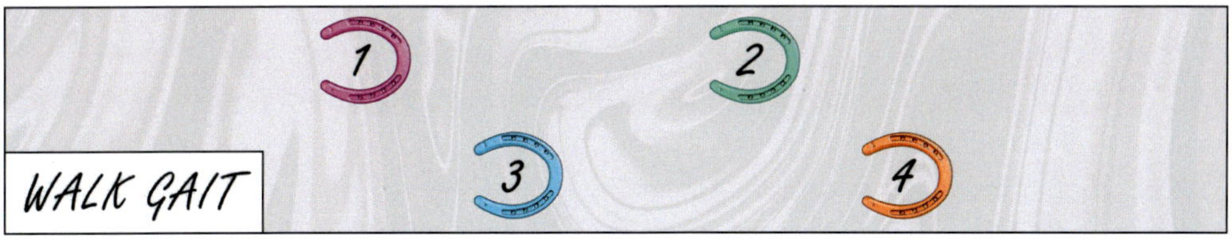

TROT

Trot has a two beat rhythm. It has a bouncing action with up to 40% of the muscular work of trotting recovered via the storage and release of elastic strain energy in ligaments, tendons and muscles of the limbs. The horse's legs move as diagonal pairs: the left hind is paired with the right foreleg and the right hind is paired with the left foreleg. A moment of suspension occurs between each diagonal pairing where no hooves are grounded.

The trot is the most expressive of the gaits, two variations of trot are passage and piaffe.

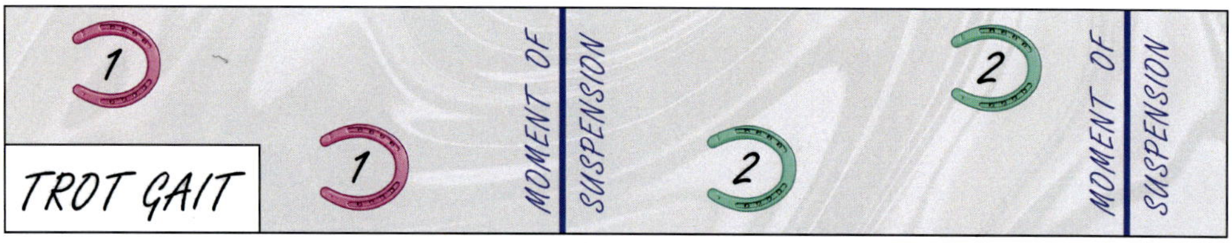

Passage is a very collected, slow, elevated and cadenced trot. It is distinguished from a collected trot by its shorter stride length, slower and heightened steps and a more accentuated flexion of the knees and hocks. The duration of the stance phases and the periods of suspension are longer than those observed in collected trot.

Piaffe, is a highly collected diagonal movement performed on the spot. Technically due to the lack of a suspension phase, piaffe is in fact not a pure form of trot.

An expressive trot has:

- A slow stride frequency and a long swing phase
- Maximal retraction and protraction of the limbs
- Maximal flexion of the hocks
- Vertical elasticity.

RISING TROT

The benefits of rising (otherwise known as posting) in trot is twofold. Firstly, it is physically easier for the rider and more comfortable than sitting to the trot. Secondly, it encourages the horse to lift his back.

To rise in trot, the rider should not push against the stirrups; she should allow the horse to assist her rise by gently pushing her out of the saddle. Her knees should remain relaxed, and the leg should be allowed to drop downwards as she rises to assist positional stability. By engaging her stomach muscles to resist being thrown out of rhythm and balance, the rider controls the up and forward trajectory of her rise. By this method it is easier to minimise the rise; therefore the rider should land lightly in the saddle by carefully controlling her descent.

If the rider actively rises by pushing down on the stirrups she will find it harder to remain in synchrony with the horse's movement and may find herself either ahead of or behind the trotting movement.

The rider should rise on a specific diagonal. The phrase 'rise and fall with the shoulder on the wall' is a useful way of remembering this. This has a biomechanical benefit when riding in a circular movement – the outside shoulder must travel further around the track than the inside shoulder. By rising as the outside shoulder is moving forward greater, freedom of movement occurs.

> 'To control how you return to the saddle in rising trot, imagine that there are drawing pins on the seat of your saddle.' Robert Hall

RIDER TIP…

Some riders find it easier to retain dynamic balance in rising trot if their upper body is inclined slightly forwards.

RIDER TIP…

In rising trot, do not push against the stirrups to rise.

RIDER TIP…

Do not straighten or set the knee in rising trot as you will fall behind the rhythm.

SITTING TROT

Sitting trot is never easily achieved nor is it comfortable until the horse is able to lift his back and step well under his torso. If the rider sits the trot before the horse is sufficiently engaged she will have the feeling of being propelled forwards from a point behind the saddle. Young horses should be ridden in rising trot only.

CANTER

Canter has a three beat rhythm with a moment of suspension which requires more effort from the horse due to its bounding action. Canter is described as left lead or right lead. When on the right rein the rider normally uses right lead canter: the leg sequence is left hind (1st beat), right hind and left foreleg diagonally paired (2nd beat) and the right foreleg (3rd beat) followed by a moment of suspension.

When on the left rein the rider normally uses left lead canter: the leg sequence is right hind (1st beat), left hind and right foreleg diagonally paired (2nd beat) and the left foreleg (3rd beat) followed by a moment of suspension.

CANTER GAIT - RIGHT REIN

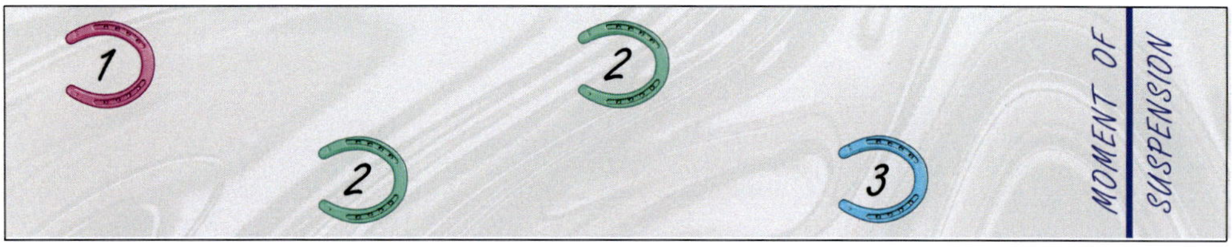

CANTER GAIT - LEFT REIN

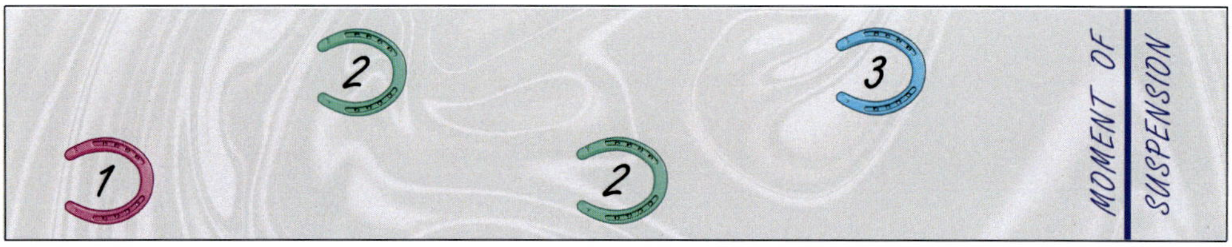

VARIATIONS WITHIN THE GAITS

There are five dressage related variations within each gait: free, working, medium, extended and collected.

FREE... Free walk is more commonly used than free trot and free canter. It is so named because the horse is free of restriction, he is moving in a way which he finds the least demanding. The free walk is similar to the purposeful walk the horse performs when walking around a field. His frame should be long and low, permitting significant over-tracking.

WORKING... The stride length of a working gait is greater than that of a collected gait and shorter than the medium version. The working gaits are active and purposeful. They are energy efficient and therefore capable of being sustained for longer periods. The horse should track up in working gaits.

MEDIUM... The medium gaits require greater impulsion and energetic effort by the horse. The stride length is longer than that of the working gaits and the horse should over-track. The horse's frame is lengthened with the back lifted. The horse should not speed up in the medium gaits but should cover more ground. Medium trot and canter should display increased elevation and cadence.

EXTENDED... The extended gaits require greater effort from the horse than the medium gaits. The horse should over-track by two or three hoof lengths. The frame is lengthened more than in the medium gaits. Trot and canter should show greater elevation and cadence than the medium gaits.

COLLECTED... In collected gaits the horse's frame is shortened as a result of increased engagement of the hind quarters and a greater arching and lifting of the back. The impression is of the haunches bearing greater weight, the forehand elevated with the neck arched and carried high. The steps are elevated and springy with shortened stride length.

THE THEORY OF THE AIDS

The aids are the means by which a rider communicates with the horse. The purpose of an aiding system is to "aid" the horse, to assist him in developing the necessary strength to carry the rider, to guide and influence him whilst retaining the fluidity and beauty of his natural movement. Anyone wishing to ride in a refined way should understand the theory of aiding, the techniques of their application and the importance of their correct timing. The rider should also have a conceptual understanding of the basic training aims and the changes they wish to action. The aids originate in the rider's mind as intentions. Once a rider has knowledge of how she can bring about the changes she wishes to make, she should unconsciously posturally communicate her intentions to the horse.

The aim of a finessed aiding system is to encourage the horse to respond actively to light, subtle aids and to become responsive to small changes in the rider's position and posture. The rider should be able to convey how they wish the horse to respond without resorting to repetition or physical exertion. The aids should never be harsh nor use excessive pressure or force. The aim is to train responsiveness and to eliminate the need for repetition in aiding.

THE ACTIVE AND THE PASSIVE AIDS

The aids can be subdivided into active and passive. The passive aids should co-ordinate with and support the effectiveness of the active aids.

THE PASSIVE AIDS

When learning, many riders are taught only the active aids, e.g. to turn by use of the inside leg and inside rein; however, it is possible for a rider to turn the horse with her body alone without using reins. A finessed aiding system uses passive aiding where possible and preferentially. It is possible for a rider to slow and stop the horse by using her body to resist the flow of the horse's movement.

The passive aids are supportive influences. The rider's position can function as a framework to contain and guide the horse. With the correct position a rider can subtly and gently direct the flow of the horse's energy, influence his speed, straightness, direction, and bend.

UNDERSTANDING THE USE OF THE PASSIVE AIDS IS CRUCIAL TO SENSITIVE AND SUBTLE AIDING.

THE BASIC FRAMEWORK...

- The rider's left shoulder and arm controls the horse's left shoulder.
- The rider's left leg controls the horse's left hind quarters.
- The rider's right shoulder and arm controls the horse's right shoulder.
- The rider's right leg controls the horse's right hind quarters.

Novice horses require greater support from a rider's passive aids than more advanced horses. The novice horse may require the rider to move the focus of the passive aids from one part of the frame to another as the novice horse is unlikely to travel in a straight line unassisted. If a rider loses contact with the horse through breaks in their 'position framework', the horse can then escape or 'fall out' through these breaks.

A REFINED AIDING SYSTEM USES CHANGES IN THE RIDING POSITION AND POSTURAL TENSION TO BEST EFFECT.

> "The rider's body should be used to support the horse. It should never be used to force the horse into a frame." Robert Hall

THE ACTIVE AIDS

The active aids originate in the rider's mind and should prepare the rider's body to react appropriately when she actions the aids. The aids of the seat should predominate and be supported by the rider's position, voice, legs, and hands. The active aids are in action for a shorter duration and are used more 'actively' than the passive aids. An example of an active aid is when both legs are applied briefly and simultaneously at the girth to support the action of the seat when asking the horse to move forwards.

The active aids, with the exception of the voice aids, consist of lightly applied pressures which are instantly released when the horse complies. Horse training differs fundamentally from the methods used to train other animals which usually utilise food treats as rewards. To reward the horse for good efforts, the rider may use her voice soothingly, may scratch him at the withers, may allow him to stretch in walk on a loose rein or may terminate the training session.

The active aids can be applied using differing amounts of rider effort and these are termed strong aids, medium strength aids and light finessed aids. All ethical riding systems should aim to use the lightest possible aids to achieve the desired response. The aids should be of short duration and the rider should give the horse time to respond.

If a rider is aiming to influence a specific leg, the duration of the aid should be very short and finely timed to influence that leg only. If the rider wishes the horse to respond instantly to a leg aid, for example to move to a faster gait, the leg aid should last under half a second, best thought off as a light touch with the calves or a more active touch if more energy is required. The use of leg aids which are hugging squeezes, lasting a second or more, will not encourage the horse to become immediately responsive and in front of the leg.

When a rider wishes to slow or stop the horse, the leg aid is of longer duration – a hugging squeeze that may last a number of seconds. This action of the legs is asking for increased engagement and balanced deceleration.

RIDER TIP...

The use of strong or forceful aids is not advised; they will work in opposition to the desired response by negatively impacting rhythm, tempo, and relaxation.

RIDER TIP...

The more inexperienced the horse, the more patience is required. It is unreasonable to expect the newly backed horse to respond instantly to aids.

THE AIDING SYSTEM IS A TWO-WAY PROCESS

For the aiding process to be effective it must be a two-way interaction. The horse should be listening attentively for guidance from the rider and in turn the rider must be willing to 'listen' to feedback from the horse. In order to facilitate a heightened ability to 'listen', the rider must remain in dynamic balance at all times and have acquired an independent seat and hands.

The sensitive rider is aware that a horse can ask questions.

> "If you are not aware that the horse is asking you a question, then you have no understanding of the concept of riding which is all about the conversation between the horse and the rider." Robert Hall

> "When you give an aid to your horse you give the indication, now you have to wait a moment for his reply: this is a question and answer game. You ask him a question and his reply will influence what you do next." Robert Hall

FINDING THE BALANCE BETWEEN OVER-RIDING AND UNDER-RIDING

> "The more one does the less one succeeds."
> Attributed to Nuno Oliveira

The ultimate goal of a finessed riding system is that the horse should require minimal aiding. When a rider is under pressure to perform, it is easy for her to make the mistake of over-aiding, particularly if the horse becomes inattentive or distracted. Overuse of the aids has a major drawback in that it will render the horse less responsive to the aids. The more the rider aids, the less the horse 'listens', and the more frustrated the rider becomes.

A common issue horse owners face is retraining a horse which is behind the leg to become more responsive. Overuse of the aids will prevent the horse from grasping the concept that he should continue to travel forward with only one aid until another request is made.

RIDER TIP…

Over-riding and over-aiding are counter-productive to the rider wishing to develop a superior level of connection with the horse.

When you give an aid and it is not complied with, why give the same aid in the same way? If the horse is not reacting to a specific aid, it is wise to examine the timing and clarity of the aid, in an attempt to find a better way of asking. Repetition of an aid that did not initiate a response from the horse can result in the horse becoming desensitised to that aid.

If a different aid is unsuccessful, try pairing the aid with a voice aid that the horse responds to in groundwork training.

If the horse does not react to a light aid and the rider then gives another aid which does not elicit a response, by repeating the aid a third or fourth time the horse learns that he need not respond to the first or second aid as a third or fourth will follow. What is being trained is a lack of responsiveness.

THE HORSE SHOULD BE TRAINED TO RESPOND TO THE FIRST AND ONLY AID.

RIDER TIP…

Always give the horse time to warm up; do not ask too much of him from the moment of mounting.

Under-riding, or insufficient rider input, also has its pitfalls as it permits the horse to continue to travel on his forehand, and as a result he becomes unbalanced and rushes.

RIDER TIP…

When riding an unreactive horse, be patient, allow time for the horse to react to lighter aids.

LEARN THE SKILL OF CEASING THE AIDS

Cessation is the key to a finessed aiding system. Learning to cease the aids is every bit as important as understanding when to use them. If a horse is in balance and in self-carriage, the rider can cease aiding until the horse requires assistance or direction. The process of training involves developing the horse's natural balance and encouraging him to be self-maintaining for a reasonable length of time.

RIDER TIP...

The less a rider intervenes the more opportunity the horse has to express his natural fluidity and rhythm.

RIDER TIP...

Good aiding is often about doing less or very little. Through experience, the rider will learn the balance between aiding and cessation.

RIDER TIP...

It is wise to avoid becoming an over-demanding rider; this can quickly cause the horse to become uncooperative.

RIDER TIP...

There is no correlation between the strength of an aid and the quality of the impulsion. Giving a stronger aid does not assure you of a stronger response to an aid.

AIDING CONSISTENCY AND TIMING

> "The correct aid applied at the wrong time will not get the correct response from the horse." Robert Hall

To enable clear communication, the aids should be applied consistently. It is necessary for the rider to develop a balanced, stable riding position to enable her to apply the aids clearly and consistently.

If a rider wishes the horse to be instantly responsive to the aids, the aids must be accurately timed. To fine tune this timing and to enable her to aid at the right moment the rider should familiarise herself with the sequence of footfalls in all gaits and improve her feel for hoof placement. In asking the horse to leg-yield the rider aims to influence the inside hind leg and ask it to travel forwards and across the outside hind leg. It is not possible to alter a leg's direction of travel once it has begun thrusting. The rider must influence the inside hind just before it begins to thrust.

RIDER TIP...

Never attempt to influence a leg while it is thrusting; the leg can only be influenced before thrusting pressure is applied by the horse.

THE COORDINATION AND ISOLATION OF THE AIDS

The skilled rider must be capable of isolating an aid and also be capable of the co-ordinated use of multiple aids. The aids used must have a common goal and be co-ordinated to achieve this goal. To use a simple analogy, when driving a car if you wish to travel you must release the brake and the handbrake.

The aim is to train the pairing of one distinct aid to a desired response as this enables the isolated use of an aid.

In order either to encourage or contain movement, the rider is required to coordinate the influences of her body position, seat, legs, and hands in a specific order. Co-ordination of the aids and separation of the aids are vital skills to learn to enable subtle influencing. It is essential that the rider wishing to ride with finesse, develops the ability to isolate and use parts of her body independently without adversely affecting her balance or accidentally moving any other parts of the body.

THE AIDS IN DETAIL

A comprehensive understanding of the aids and their application is essential for finessed riding skills. The rider should first understand these before progressing to the other chapters which specifically detail the half-halt and rein-back etc.

A horse is sensitive to light pressure and because of this the aids utilise the natural reactions of the horse to pressure. Aids should be applied as lightly as possible and be of short duration, ceasing when the horse complies. There are many variations of these basic influences. The aim of an aiding system is to facilitate clear communication and to assist the horse in responding promptly and appropriately. An aiding system must work in harmony with the rider's position and the natural movements of the horse. Good aiding will assist the horse in developing greater strength and enhance his movements.

TO CREATE HARMONY... THE AIDS, THE RIDING POSITION AND THE HORSE'S MOVEMENTS MUST BE CLOSELY AND INSEPARABLY INTERLINKED.

The horse is responsive to any changes in rider position, postural tension and weight distribution. The rider should aim to sit as quietly as possible in the saddle minimising any unnecessary movements. The rider must be capable of carrying her weight equally distributed over both seatbones enabling her to action subtle weight aids. The weight aids are the central part of an aiding system.

The development of a co-operative partnership increases the horse's willingness to respond to light and subtle aids.

Changes in the rider's postural tension can influence the flow of the horse's forward movement. The more the rider is able to control the horse by the use of her seat and body tension, the more subtle her influences can become.

The rider can influence the horse with her energy and thoughts; this influence can be either positive or negative. By simply imagining cantering when trotting it is possible to energise the trot.

AIDING SHOULD SUPPORT THE FOUR BASIC AIMS IN TRAINING...

TO PRESERVE FREE FORWARD MOVEMENT... The horse which has not yet been ridden will naturally move forward rhythmically and freely. If the rider adopts a good position and can maintain dynamic balance, she will be capable of preserving the natural beauty of his gaits.

TO ENCOURAGE OVERTRACKING... The rider should be aware of the place on which the hooves land so that she can assist the horse in tracking up. He should be encouraged to develop the strength to over-track. If he is not tracking up, he is not using his hind quarters and back correctly.

TO ENCOURAGE LIFTING OF THE BACK... The horse's spine can be compared to a beam which has support at each end. Unlike a wooden beam, the horse's spine has a slight natural dip in the middle. When the weight of a saddle and rider is placed upon this area the tendency to hollow is increased. The rider must encourage the horse to lift his back and be careful not to overwork him.

The rider should encourage the horse to make a bridge of his back. This is achieved by encouraging the horse to step well under his body, especially in half-halts and halts.

TO TRAVEL STRAIGHT AND TO ENCOURAGE SUPPLENESS... The horse is encouraged to develop symmetrical body balance through correct training.

BASIC RULES FOR AIDING

> "Never surprise your horse with an aid." Robert Hall

- The impulsive aids should be applied before the restraining aids ... 'always use the leg before the hand'.
- The impulsive aids should predominate, and their influence should be far greater than the restraining aids... 'more leg than hand'.
- Focus on the development of the horse's hind quarters... 'ride from the back of the horse to the front'.
- Never attempt to pull the horse together by the reins... 'never pull the horse into an outline'.
- All aids must work towards a single intention and not be contradictory. 'Don't confuse the horse.'

THE BASIC AIDING FRAMEWORK

A horse can be trained to respond to almost any aid. A good aiding system should be designed to enable layers of influence to be built upon a sound basic structure. A logical system is more easily understood, and easily replicated.

Robert Hall believed that the practice of riding from inside leg to outside hand was too simplistic and found that it did not work well for some horses. The rider's body should be used to guide and support the horse where and when he needs support. If the rider uses her aids effectively the horse will find it easy to respond correctly. The use of a basic framework provides a solid foundation for subtle influences to be overlaid.

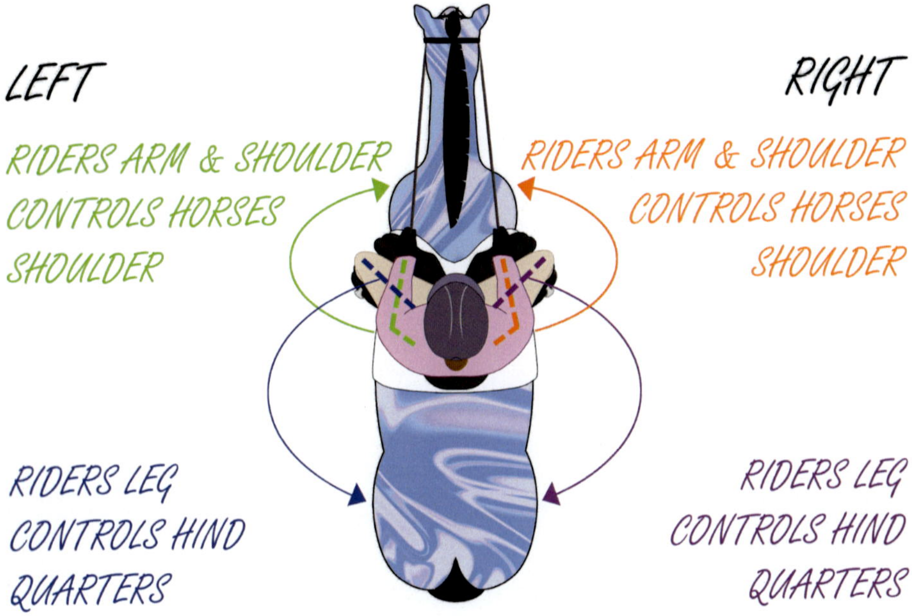

THE BASIC AIDING FRAMEWORK IS:

- The rider's left shoulder and arm controls the horse's left shoulder.
- The rider's left leg controls the horse's left hind quarters.
- The rider's right shoulder and arm controls the horse's right shoulder.
- The rider's right leg controls the horse's right hind quarters.

THE AIDS

GOOD AIDING INVOLVES CAREFUL PREPARATION TO ENSURE SMOOTH EXECUTION

Before detailing all the different rider influences, it is important to mention that horses are capable of recognising a regularly repeated chain of events. For example, if the rider has a set preparation before an aid is applied, the horse may make a transition before the aid is given. This is not disobedience and should not be punished. The thinking rider uses this equine intelligence to their advantage and as a means of refining the aids.

The aids can be used individually but more commonly they are coordinated with other aids and influences. The rider can subtly control the horse's energy, rhythm, forwardness, impulsion and speed by carefully balancing the active aids which are generated by the active use of the rider's lower back, seatbones and legs, with the containing function applied by the rider's seat, torso and thighs.

The seat aids should predominate and should be assisted and supported by the other aids and influences. Key to refined aiding is the rider's ability to perform separate actions with each of her seatbones, legs and hands.

THE WEIGHT AIDS

> "The horse will always try to position himself under the rider's centre of gravity." Author Unknown.

The weight aids are the primary influences. The easiest way to understand is to consider how someone carrying a heavy rucksack upon their shoulders might react if the rucksack slipped to one side. If it moved to the left, it would be necessary for her to move left to restore the rucksack's centre of gravity and her balance.

The horse will always try to position himself under the rider's centre of gravity; by moving her centre of gravity the rider can therefore move the horse.

It is unsurprising that the horse responds to subtle changes in the distribution of the rider's weight considering the effect of the combined weight of the saddle and rider. The importance of the weight aids in a finessed aiding system cannot be overemphasised.

To enable the horse to feel subtle weight aids, the rider must be capable of sitting centrally with their weight evenly placed over the horse's spine.

The weight aids are actioned by small changes in the rider's centre of gravity and by careful weighting of the seatbones and/or the stirrups. A weight aid should be subtle and barely discernible. The rider should place sufficient weight on the seatbone to action a response but not affect the horse's balance. Some riders place a little pressure on the stirrup iron via the ball of their foot, which can be sufficient to action a weight aid in a seatbone.

The rider's upper body should be unaffected by the application of weight aids. Her shoulders should remain level and her upper body should retain good postural alignment. Her waist must lengthen as weight is dropped down her leg and she should not collapse at the waist.

The weight aids can be used to:

- Indicate changes of direction.
- Ride circles, loops and turns.
- Ask for bend.
- Assist in lateral movements.
- Ask for right or left flexion at the poll.

THE WEIGHT AIDS ON A CIRCLE

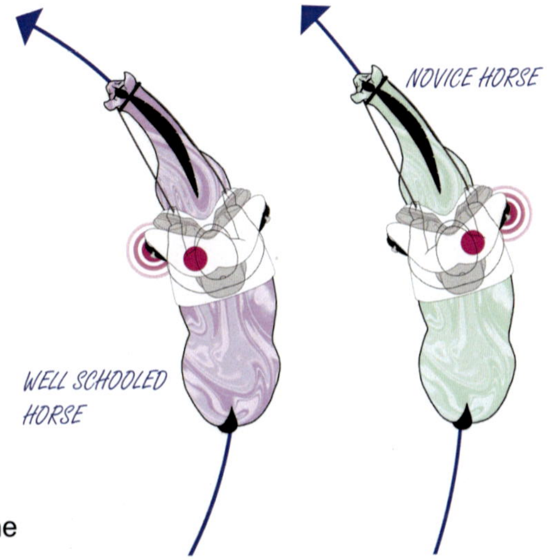

When riding circles the aim is to encourage the horse to carry his weight equally over the left and right halves of his body thus assisting his balance when turning.

In nature, the horse turns by bringing his inside foreleg towards his midline and leans over it. When circling a novice horse, to discourage him from leaning over his inside foreleg and encourage him to transfer weight to his outside foreleg, the rider may have to place a little more of her weight to the outside. She may have to place more weight on her outside seatbone and on the outside stirrup.

When circling a well-schooled horse, a little more weight should be over the inside seatbone, and the rider should place a little more weight on her inside stirrup. The rider should feel the pressure of the stirrup pushing back against the ball of her inside foot.

THE SEAT AIDS AND THE INFLUENCES OF THE SEAT

> "Over-use of the seat prevents the rider from gleaning valuable feedback information from the horse." Robert Hall

The aim when refining the aids is for the majority of the aids to be delivered via the seat with the hands and legs used sparingly. Through a process of refining the aids, the ultimate aim is for the seat to be the origin of at least 90% of the aids. Good aiding involves early intervention and does not rely on overuse of the aids.

If the rider's seat replaces many of the functions of her hands, she is then able to communicate on a more open channel to the horse, facilitating more subtle adjustments.

The basic influence of the seat detailed in Chapter 4 includes: allowing with the seat; the lightened seat, the restricting seat and the use of the seat to encourage forward movement.

TO FINESSE THE USE OF THE SEAT, THE RIDER MUST BE CAPABLE OF ADVANCING EACH HIP INDEPENDENTLY. THIS CAN BE PRACTISED...PLACE A HEAVY HARDBACK BOOK ON A TABLE LEAVING A COUPLE OF INCHES OVERHANGING. STANDING IN RIDING ALIGNMENT, LEGS APART, KNEES SOFTLY BENT WITH THE TOES POSITIONED A FEW INCHES BACK FROM

THE TABLE LEDGE, PUSH THE BOOK BACK ON TO THE TABLE BY ADVANCING EACH HIP. THE FEET MUST REMAIN GROUNDED, THE HEELS SHOULD NOT RISE.

A GOOD SEAT, A SECURE RIDING POSITION AND A FLEXIBLE PELVIS ARE NECESSARY TO ACTION THE FOLLOWING:

RIDER TIP...

A good way to assist the development of an independent seat is to ride without rein contact, performing turns, transitions, and lateral work without any assistance from the reins.

THE SEATBONES ALONE CAN BE USED TO TURN THE HORSE... If the rider combines the use of a weighted inside seatbone and advances her outside seatbone to turn the outside shoulder, she can turn the horse solely with her seat and the weight aids. The outside seatbone can be used to control the size of the circle, the tightness of a turn and can replace the role of the outside rein. The inside seatbone can initiate a turn, thus replacing the use of the inside rein.

THE SEATBONES CAN BE USED TO MOVE THE HORSE LATERALLY... By placing a little more weight on the inside seatbone and using the seatbone actively in the direction of travel, it is possible to direct the horse laterally. In leg-yield the action of the inside seatbone is towards the horse's outside shoulder.

RIDER TIP...

Relaxed buttocks will assist the rider's range of pelvic movements.

THE LEG AIDS

The leg aids support and assist the seat aids. They should be used sensitively. If not, and used roughly, the horse will hold his ribcage tightly, making it very difficult for the rider to create a good quality bend. The horse's sides, much like the rider's ribcage, are not protected by thick layers of musculature or thick skin. His skin contains many pain and pressure receptors and gentle leg aids should be sufficient to action a response. The rider's legs should drape against the horse's sides, the aids being actioned by the inside of her calves. The development of 'sensitive legs' is equally as important as the development of 'sensitive hands'. Gripping and stiffness in the legs are insensitive legs. The rider should aim to receive much important feedback via her legs.

THE HORSE SHOULD BE RESPONSIVE TO THE LEG AIDS

> "The legs should be used in such a way as to convey the energy with which the horse should respond." Robert Hall

The leg aid consists of gentle pressure and its timed release. It is important that the legs be used in easily differentiated ways to action different responses. Active leg aids can be actioned via both legs simultaneously or by one leg.

The rider should develop a stable leg position to enable accurate aiding. A swinging lower leg will prevent the refined use of the leg aids. The leg aids should harmoniously coordinate with the use of the seat to achieve elegant responses.

The horse should respond with energy to the forward aids and the aids for transitions. The better trained horse will respond more immediately. The newly backed horse may have a significant time lag before he responds.

Normally, the inside of the calves should lie against the horse's sides; however there are occasions when keeping the legs off the horse's sides by millimetres rather than centimetres can prove beneficial. To resensitise horses which have become unresponsive to leg aids, riding with the leg off can make the horse much more sensitive to the leg aids when applied.

Riders are often incorrectly advised use 'more leg' to solve many riding issues. If less leg is applied with correct timing a more instantaneous response can be achieved. If the rider chooses the path of increasing the strength of her leg aids, she will reach a point where she physically cannot apply a stronger aid.

MORE LEG DOES NOT GUARANTEE A BETTER RESPONSE...THERE IS NO CORRELATION BETWEEN THE STRENGTH OF THE LEG AID AND THE QUALITY OF THE RESPONSE.

The horse should be trained to be in front of the leg and willingly respond to the action of light aids.

If the horse is not responsive there are issues which may be the cause:

- The horse may be physically unable to comply, if he is lame or arthritic.
- The rider may be blocking his forward movement.
- The horse may be unresponsive to the aids as a result of them being overused.
- The aids may not be timed correctly.
- The horse may require more assistance with his balance to enable him to comply responsively.

RIDER TIP...

Before applying a leg aid, allow the thigh and calf to relax before applying the calf against the horse. The heel should not be lifted.

RIDER TIP...

The horse should be trained to react to the tensing of the calves, with the calves relaxing when not aiding.

FOUR DIFFERENT LEG POSITIONS... FOUR DIFFERENT RESPONSES

The leg can be applied to different areas on the horse's side to action different responses: in front of the girth, on the girth, behind the girth and further behind the girth.

Horses may vary in the exact location of these four reactive areas. The shorter-backed horse generally has a closer grouping. It may take time to find the precise location of these areas; luckily horses are able to generalise and will try to respond correctly.

This system is logical. The different leg positions ask a horse to change some aspect of his movement.

When the rider is correctly aligned, with reference to her ear, shoulder, hip and heel, her leg position is termed 'on the girth', although more often in reality it is behind the girth. Position 1 is the non-aiding, resting leg position and the position used for activating or 'go forward' aids; walk on and trot on. Saddle construction, positioning and girth designs may vary but the rider's alignment should not.

Position 2 is located in front of Position 1 nearer the horse's elbow. The rider's leg is moved slightly forward. Use this leg position to lengthen the horse's stride. There exists a biomechanical explanation for this application to lengthen the stride. Although it is possible to lengthen a horse's stride by other means, use Position 2 as it is easily understood by the horse.

When initially training a turn and lateral work, the outside leg can utilise Position 2 as a direct means of asking the horse to move his shoulders inwards and over. The leg is used with directional pressure.

Position 3 is situated behind Position 1. In position 3, the leg is moved a little further back on the horse's side. This position influences the hind legs. It is used to ask for lateral movements, such as leg-yield. The aid should be timed to best influence the horse's inside hind leg to assist it in crossing over the outside hind leg. Position 3 is also used to ask for increased engagement. If the rider's legs are stretched down before aiding it indicates that the rider wishes the horse to lift his back.

Position 3 can be used to control the quarters. It is used when the quarters drift outwards when circling. Position 3 helps the quarters to remain in the correct position when performing pirouettes, half-pass, renvers and travers.

Position 4 is a little further back than Position 3. I use Position 4 to guide the quarters in rein-back. It can also be effectively utilised to control the quarters in pirouettes, half-pass, renvers and travers.

SPECIFIC LEG AIDS

The legs may be used in unison, performing the same actions or different actions, or may be required to aid the horse independently of each other.

The legs assist the seat to:

- Create forward movement.
- Activate the hindquarters (impulsion).
- Indicate direction.
- Support the horse's frame.
- Contain the horse's movement.
- Slow and stop.
- Assist the horse to bend..
- Perform lateral manoeuvres.

TO ACTIVATE... The legs are applied as one, in unison, to support an activating seat aid. The legs should indicate the energy with which the rider wishes the horse to respond.

To ask the horse to trot on, the legs should be applied as one in unison to support an activating seat aid, but with more urgency and energy than is required for walk on, which is conveyed by the use of slightly more pressure and a briefer application.

TO ASK FOR MORE ENERGY OR IMPULSION... Use only the inside leg to support the seat in asking for more impulsion. This distinguishes the aid from that of walk on and trot on.

TO CREATE BEND... The rider's inside leg should support a weight aid by the use of the inside seatbone to assist in the creation of bend. By engagement of the muscles on the inside of the thigh and calf, her leg becomes pillarlike. The action of the inside seatbone and leg is towards the horse's spine. The horse is asked to bend around the rider's inside leg and to rotate his ribcage to the outside of the bend.

TO TURN AND CHANGE DIRECTION... The rider's outside leg can assist the seat and hands in turning and changing direction.

TO HALT, OR TRANSITION TO A SLOWER GAIT... The rider closes her legs in Position 1 against the horse's sides. She should apply her legs for 3 to 4 seconds to help contain the momentum of the movement and to support the actions of the restricting seat. Her stomach and thigh muscles are used to support the constant action of the legs.

TO MOVE THE HORSE LATERALLY... The leg can be used to support the seat's action in moving the horse laterally. The action of the leg is in the direction of travel.

TO ASK FOR GREATER ENGAGEMENT... Leg Position 3 is used to ask for increased engagement. If the leg is stretched downwards before aiding it can indicate that the rider wishes the horse to lift his back. The action of the leg must be combined with the lightening of the rider's seat to achieve the best result.

THE VOICE

The voice is a much underused and misunderstood tool. It can be used to encourage, soothe and reward the horse. It is necessary when giving commands. In training, the horse responds to voice aids when being lunged and long-reined. The rider can utilise these commands by pairing them with light aids to assist the horse in grasping the meaning of the aids.

In dressage tests, the use of the voice results in the deduction of points. The novice horse competing in strange surroundings would greatly benefit from the soothing voice of his rider. It would benefit the horse if this rule were to be relaxed in unaffiliated competitions.

THE HANDS

The hand aids should be of secondary importance and should be used to support the aids of the seat and legs. The hands should not be overused. The timing of the hand aids are crucial; early intervention to adjust the horse's balance and tempo is key. If the rider can act the instant that she detects the horse losing balance, subtle use of the hand aids may be sufficient to assist the horse in regaining his balance. The longer the horse travels out of balance the more rebalancing he will require.

HAND AIDS TIPS...

- ALLOW WITH THE HANDS
- NEVER CLENCH THE HAND TIGHTLY AROUND THE REIN
- NEVER RIDE WITH THE REINS SO SHORT THAT THE HORSE IS FORCED INTO A FRAME
- HAND AIDS MUST BE LIGHT AND SUBTLE
- THE HANDS SHOULD BE CAPABLE OF WORKING BOTH IN UNISON AND INDEPENDENTLY OF EACH OTHER
- HAND AIDS MUST BE OF SHORT DURATION
- NEVER PULL BACK ON THE REINS

THE HAND AIDS

The hands can operate in a number of ways: ALLOWING, NOT-ALLOWING, SUPPORTING, REGULATING, INDICATING DIRECTION AND ASSISTING WITH RELAXION IN THE MOUTH AND POLL.

ALLOWING ... The most important action of the hands is in allowing the horse to stretch forward into the contact and allowing him to lengthen his frame in the medium and extended gaits. Restricting hands will create numerous problems for both horse and rider.

NOT-ALLOWING... Having stressed the importance of the allowing hand, the non-allowing hand is a useful tool when USED MOMENTARILY. The non-allowing hand is used in conjunction with the legs and seat to rebalance the horse in downward transitions, the half-halt, the halt and rein-back. The hands or the fingers in contact with the reins are closed briefly. The hands or fingers should release any tension when the horse responds but the thumb must not release to the point that it allows the reins to slip through. THE HANDS MUST NEVER TRAVEL BACKWARDS IN A PULL.

SUPPORTING... Horses are naturally inclined to bend at the base of the neck. When turning, the rider wishes to encourage bending throughout the length of the neck. The outside hand is used to help support the amount of bend in turns, circles, lateral work and pirouettes.

REGULATING... The regulating hand aid is used to control speed. Normally only the outside hand is used to support the aids of the seat and legs to slow the horse. This can be achieved by a series of squeezes on the rein.

OPENING THE REIN... The inside hand can be moved away from the horse's neck to indicate direction in turns. This action can be used in the early training of leg-yield, turn on the forehand, turn on the haunches, walk pirouettes, full-pass and half-pass. Initially the hand may be moved approximately up to 4 inches from its original position. Over time the distance can be reduced.

INDICATING DIRECTION... To support the weight aids, the aids of the seat and the leg, the inside rein is normally squeezed more than once to indicate a change of direction.

ASSISTING WITH RELAXATION OF THE MOUTH AND POLL... The hands can be used in conjunction with the seat and the legs to encourage the horse to work forwards whilst relaxing into the contact. By very gently vibrating one rein, the jaw and tongue can be encouraged to release tension. Normally this vibrational action is used on the rein which contains tension and importantly no backwards hand action should be used. Less vibration is more effective than more vibration. It is wise to start with the tiniest possible movement and build up to a level that results in a release of tension in the horse.

RIDER TIP...

The horse is the best judge of good hands and provides the most useful feedback on contact. If you wish to improve the quality of your contact, it is essential to remove tack which closes the mouth.

THE INFLUENCES OF THE HEAD, THE SHOULDERS, THE ABDOMEN AND LOWER BACK

The rider's influences and aids should work in harmony towards a common goal. The rider should be aware of the importance of the following:

THE HEAD... The horse can readily detect changes in the positioning of the rider's head. This is unsurprising when considering its weight is around 10 lbs. Riders should look in the direction that they wish to travel. Looking downwards negatively impacts upon the rider's posture and balance.

In flatwork and dressage the rider should not look too far ahead, she should keep her nose in line with her sternum. When turning and circling, it is best to look no further than the next step. If the rider is looking at the end point of the manoeuvre she will negatively influence the horse's path and may cause it to fall in or hurry.

RIDER TIP...

When jumping, riders can achieve tighter turns by looking towards their next fence.

RIDER TIP...

If a horse tends to fall in, directing your gaze over the horse's outside ear can prove helpful. Conversely if the horse tends to fall out the rider should direct her gaze over his inside ear.

THE SHOULDERS... The horse can detect changes in the positioning of the rider's shoulders. The rider can turn the horse without reins by turning her head and shoulders. The correct positioning of the shoulders in circles and lateral manoeuvres will greatly assist the horse in performing with greater accuracy.

Circles can be improved by active use of the waist. The rider's outside shoulder can be advanced and the inside shoulder positioned slightly backwards by directing the focus on the use of the waist to move the shoulders. A smaller circle requires greater movement of the waist.

The positioning of the rider's shoulders slightly behind vertical alignment can be utilised to help control speed and to control horses who rush. The rider should not allow her pelvic position to move and inadvertently action a driving aid.

To assist in riding accurate pirouettes and in maintaining rhythm and balance in medium and extended gaits, the shoulders can be positioned slightly behind vertical alignment.

THE ABDOMEN AND LUMBAR REGION... Key to the correct functioning of the riding position and the effectiveness of the aids is the interaction between the muscles of the front and back of the rider's torso. The lower back and abdomen influence the rider's seat, her pelvic tilt, and the action of her seatbones. They play a crucial role in maintaining the correct pelvic position in motion. They are also an essential cog in the mechanism which allows the flow of the horse's free forward movement and the containment of it.

TRANSITIONS

> "True collection will not be achieved unless the proper fundamentals are in place at the earliest stage in the transitions." Robert Hall

> "Any errors made by the horse are caused by the rider, who either failed to prepare the horse correctly or did not ask clearly enough." Robert Hall

Good preparation is key to smooth transitions, the horse should never be surprised by an aid. When required, the horse's balance should be adjusted before transitions.

ALL TRANSITIONS SHOULD AIM TO MAINTAIN THE HORSE IN UPHILL BALANCE.

Uphill balance should be maintained when transitioning to slower gaits and faster gaits. The horse should not fall on his forehand in transitions. In every transition the rider should encourage the horse to lift and round his back and to step well under his body. It is generally easier for the horse to retain balance when transitioning to a faster gait. When transitioning to a slower gait he requires greater rebalancing input from the rider. The half-halt is key to rebalancing the horse.

ALL TRANSITIONS TO SLOWER GAITS SHOULD BE RIDDEN FORWARDS, RETAINING FORWARD ENERGY.

TO TRANSITION FROM HALT TO WALK… the rider applies both legs in unison acting momentarily in Position 1 with an activating seat aid.

TO TRANSITION FROM WALK TO TROT… the legs should be applied in unison to support an activating seat aid using a method similar to that used to initiate walk. More urgency and energy is conveyed by the use of slightly more pressure and a briefer application.

TO TRANSITION FROM TROT TO WALK… the rider should first commence sitting trot, using half-halts to rebalance the horse before closing her legs inwards in Position 1. The legs should be applied constantly for 3 to 4 seconds to help contain the momentum of the movement and to support the actions of a restricting seat. Her stomach and thigh muscles are used to support the action of the legs. Her hands should then close on the reins and should release the moment she feels the horse commence the transition to walk.

TO TRANSITION FROM CANTER TO TROT… this transition is very similar to trot to walk. The rider must ensure that the horse's hind legs are reaching well underneath his body. The propulsive power of the hind legs must be controlled to ensure that the horse is not pushed on to his forehand.

TO TRANSITION FROM CANTER TO WALK… the rider should ride as in to canter to trot but with the greater use of rebalancing and restraining aids.

TO TRANSITION FROM TROT TO CANTER… a good canter transition is more easily achieved if the horse is travelling in a well-balanced and rhythmical trot. The rider should use sitting trot for a few strides before commencing the aids. Half-halts are the most effective way to prepare him to strike off into canter. Most horses have a preferred canter lead, which they may try to select if the aid applied is somewhat ambiguous. For this reason it is important that the rider be clear in her asking.

The horse should be rebalanced via half-halts before being asked to transition into canter. To ensure clear aiding, the riding position and bodyweight distribution should be checked before and maintained during the aid for canter. The aid for canter starts with the horse being asked to flex slightly to the inside at the poll; a slight weighting of the inside seatbone occurs before the inside leg (in Position 1) and the seat are used in unison. The inside leg acts as an inwards nudge and the inside seatbone is advanced as the seat acts as a momentary driving aid.

Do not allow the horse to speed up in trot to transition into canter. The horse should be encouraged to instantly respond to the canter aid. If he is permitted to trot hurriedly he will be unbalanced when transitioning.

COUNTER CANTER

The main purpose of counter-canter is to develop the horse's straightness. The aid for counter-canter can be most easily thought of as asking for canter right when on the left rein and vice versa. The horse should be counter-flexed (his nose to the outside of the arena) with the weight aid placed on the outside seatbone. The rider asks for canter by using her outside leg (Position 1) and seat in unison. The outside leg acts as an inwards nudge and the outside seatbone is advanced as her seat acts as a momentary driving aid. The rider should maintain the riding position that reflects the horse's lead, not the direction of travel.

RIDER TIP...

Do not throw away the contact when transitioning to a faster gait in the hope of assisting the horse. This action will not support the horse in retaining an uphill balance.

COLLECTED, MEDIUM AND EXTENDED GAITS

MEDIUM GAITS

The medium gaits require greater impulsion and energetic effort from the horse. The stride length is longer than that of the working equivalent. The horse should over-track, round his back and lengthen his frame. He should cover more ground in medium gaits. The rider must control the rhythm to prevent the horse from travelling too hurriedly. Trot and canter should show increased elevation, and cadence.

FOR MEDIUM WALK... the aids are largely seat aids, timed to influence each foreleg, the lower back actions momentary driving aids by alternately advancing each seatbone. The left seat bone's action is timed to influences the left foreleg, the right seatbone influences the right foreleg. The rider's hands must allow the horse to lengthen his frame. When actioning aids, the rider's legs are positioned forwards in Position 2. The aim is to train the horse to continue in medium walk with minimal aiding, some horses may need regular repetition of these aids.

FOR MEDIUM TROT... both legs are actively applied as one in Position 2 to support a momentary driving seat aid. The hands must allow the horse to lengthen his frame. Some horses may require the aids to be repeated to maintain the required effort.

FOR MEDIUM CANTER... the inside leg is applied with energy to support a momentary driving seat aid. The hands must allow the horse to lengthen his frame.

EXTENDED GAITS

In contrast to the medium gaits, the extended gaits require greater strength and effort from the horse. The horse must be capable of maintaining medium gaits before he will have the required strength to perform the extended gaits. The horse should over-track significantly. His frame is further lengthened. Trot and canter should show greater elevation, and cadence.

FOR EXTENDED GAITS... the aids are similar to their medium counterpart but are applied with greater purpose, energy and intention. The horse should be allowed greater freedom to lengthen his frame, but importantly he should not be permitted to drop on to his forehand.

COLLECTED GAITS

In collected gaits the horse's frame is shortened by the increased engagement of the hind quarters and the greater arching and lifting of his back. The haunches should appear to be bearing greater weight, the forehand should be elevated, the neck arched and carried high. The steps are shortened, elevated, elastic and springy.

FOR COLLECTED GAITS... The rider should place her legs back to Position 3 and use them to support the actions of a lightened restricting seat. The horse is encouraged to lift his back and to step underneath himself. The lightened seat assists the horse in shortening his frame, flexing his lumbosacral joint, stepping underneath himself and moving his centre of gravity backwards to assist his balance. The restricting seat supported by the actions of the upper body and reins assist the rider in controlling and containing the energy of the horse.

THE HALT, THE HALF-HALT AND REIN-BACK

Two of the most important aspects of riding is mastering the transition to halt and mastering the half-halt. The correct execution of the combined use of activating aids and restraining aids will rebalance the horse and support him in transferring his centre of gravity and assist him in lightening his forehand.

The key to riding the halt, the half-halt and the rein-back is never to lose the forward momentum and intention.

THE HALT

> "The key to skilful riding is to ride the halt correctly." Robert Hall

> "The rider must allow the horse to step under in the halt and the half-halt." Robert Hall

A correct halt is difficult to achieve and is not to be confused with bringing the horse to a standstill. Robert Hall placed great emphasis on the importance of mastering the halt. The instruction given was *'prepare to ride forwards into halt'.* The quality of the halt is affected by the rider's forward intention and by her ability to allow the horse to lift and round his back. Sufficient activity and forwardness is needed to assist the horse in stepping under his body and to help him halt whilst distributing his weight with an uphill balance. The halt should not appear to have occurred abruptly. It requires the horse to be working in balance, and to be quietly accepting the contact. A horse that pulls or leans on the contact cannot halt in the correct manner. To ensure a smooth transition to halt, the horse must be prepared by using half-halts.

The horse should halt squarely; his front feet and back feet should stop in imaginary parallel lines. The aim in halt is to ensure the horse remains immobile, attentive, on the bit and ready to work actively if asked. It is wise when training to ask the horse to remain immobile in halt for different durations before riding him forwards in walk, trot or canter. Note that in competition dressage the horse should remain immobile in halt whilst the rider salutes the judge.

HOW TO RIDE THE HALT

THE HANDS SHOULD NEVER PULL BACKWARDS IN HALT. THE HORSE SHOULD BE PERMITTED TO TAKE THE RIDER'S HANDS FORWARDS TO ASSIST HIM IN THE LIFTING AND ROUNDING OF HIS BACK.

TO HALT, THE RIDER SHOULD COMBINE THE USE OF ACTIVATING AND RESTRAINING AIDS.

In trot, the rider should ride into halt from a sitting trot as this is the most effective way of using the restraining influences of her body. Passive aiding is used to assist the horse in travelling in a straight line in the strides preceding the halt. The horse should be rebalanced by the use of one or more half-halts. The rider should keep her weight evenly distributed and be attentive to any deviation from the straight path.

The horse should be ridden forwards into halt. Both legs should activate the hind quarters as the restraining aids are applied. The seat and the rider's body slow and contain the horse's movement. Her hands should then close on the reins to filter and softly contain the forward momentum. The hand should not be fixed nor pull against the horse. The rider should not have the feeling of the horse becoming heavier in her hands.

The rider should lighten her seat whilst ensuring her lumbar spine is sufficiently soft and supple to assist the horse to lift his back. She should stretch her body upwards whilst engaging the muscles of the front of the torso and the tops of her thighs to maintain correct alignment during deceleration.

As the horse commences the halt, he should be permitted to take the rider's hands up, forward and round to assist him in lifting his back and stepping under. The rider should focus on the feeling of his hindlegs stepping under. It is important in halting to ask the horse to bring his legs as far under his centre of mass as he can as this enables him to spring lightly out of the halt when asked.

If one hind leg does not step up sufficiently, for example the left leg, the rider's left leg should react quickly to ask the horse to step under. Once the horse is immobile, her hands should retain a soft elastic connection to the horse's mouth; the joints of her fingers should be relaxed. The horse should remain immobile, attentive and on the bit as required. If the rider retains tension in her hands the horse could interpret this as asking for rein-back.

If the horse halts squarely with his hind legs disengaged this indicates that the rider did not soften her lower back sufficiently or at the right moment.

RIDER TIP...

It is wise to avoid the habit of halting only at the end of each session and the habit of immediately dropping the reins after the horse halts.

RIDER TIP...

The correct halt should not involve a loss of forward energy. The rider should have the feeling that the horse would move forwards immediately if asked.

RIDER TIP...

Do not give the horse an opportunity to lean on the bit going into a halt.

THE HALF-HALT

The half-halt is a hardly visible moderated version of the halt. It is a balancing tool used to prepare the horse for movements and transitions. This aid will require to be used more than any other during a schooling session by the rider unless she is riding an exceptionally well-trained and well-balanced horse. The half-halt can only be effectively actioned if the rider is sitting in the saddle. It involves the co-ordinated action of the seat, the legs and the hands, to ask the horse to move his centre of balance backwards and to lighten his forehand. Half-halts should be of short duration. There should be no backward pull, nor a prolonged squeeze with the legs. A series of half-halts can be an effective tool to rebalance the novice horse.

A well-executed half-halt will…

- Alert the horse that the rider is about to make a request.
- Improve the balance of the horse.
- Assist the horse in lightening his forehand.
- Generate impulsion.
- Assist with the engagement of the haunches.

HOW TO RIDE THE HALF-HALT

RIDER TIP…

A well-executed half-halt should be barely visible.

RIDER TIP…

The elastic connection of the hands to the horse's mouth must be retained.

To ride a half-halt the rider uses a moderated lesser version of the aids used for halt which are discontinued the instant the horse responds. The use of the activating aids should precede the restraining aids. One or both hands may be used and the fingers are relaxed the instant the horse responds.

The legs and seat are used to create forward energy. The rider's body, legs and seat ask the horse to lift his back and then travel forwards, having been rebalanced. The seat should be lightened, and the upper body stretched upwards to assist the horse in lifting his back and in stepping under. The horse should feel rebalanced, lighter in the forehand and less reliant on the reins.

For the half-halt to be effective and barely visible, the horse must be in front of the leg. The aim is to train the horse towards a very lightly applied half-halt that only lasts for the duration of the stance phase of the specific leg or legs that the rider wishes to influence.

Eventually, as the aids are finessed, the half-halt can be achieved by a moderated version of this description.

THE TIMING OF THE HALF-HALT

For a half-halt to be effective it has to be timed accurately. The half-halt utilises a momentary increase in the stance phase of the gait. The rider aims to influence the horse's leg when it touches down on the ground early in the stance phase.

When trotting, the half-halt should coincide with the moment a diagonal pair of limbs touch the ground. In canter, the half-halt should coincide with the touching down of the diagonal pair of limbs (the second beat of the canter). The choice of this moment encourages the horse to utilise the breaking forces of his front leg and to increase the upwards and backwards force to assist him in retaining an uphill balance.

The half-halt should never be timed to coincide with a thrusting hind leg. This will result in the horse coming against the bit. The half-halt should never be actioned when the hind leg is in the swing phase; this will cause the horse to shorten his stride and set down his leg prematurely. This results in a loss of rhythm and balance.

RIDER TIP...

It is better to relax the fingers and repeat the aid than close the hands for too long.

RIDER TIP...

The timing of the release of the half-halt is as crucial as the timing of the aid itself.

RIDER TIP...

The application of a half-halt of long duration is never advised as it will prove to be counterproductive.

REIN-BACK

Stepping backwards in-hand or under-saddle is termed 'backing-up'. It is useful to be able to move a horse backwards and all horses should be capable of moving backwards when asked.

Rein-back is a specific rearward movement which is always performed from halt. The horse travels backwards in a straight line by moving his legs as diagonal pairs in a 2 beat rhythm. It does not have a moment of suspension and should be performed rhythmically.

The aim is to assist the horse, by utilising flexion of the lumbosacral joint, to lift his back and move fluidly backwards without hollowing or rushing. It is utilised in training to place the horse more upon his haunches.

The horse should remain on the bit whilst retaining the capability of moving forwards when asked.

HOW TO RIDE A REIN-BACK

The key to a good rein-back is to start from a good halt. The horse should be relaxed and quietly accepting the contact. There should be no backward pull on the reins. Fine timing of the aids is necessary to perform the rein-back smoothly. The rider transfers her weight slightly towards the front of the seatbones and lightens weight at the back of her seatbones. The rider's legs travel backwards on the horse's sides to guide him.

RIDER TIP...

Be wary of teaching the rein-back to nappy horses. It is best to resolve backward thinking issues first.

The rider's body should indicate the direction of movement. She gives a light squeeze with both legs and then closes her fingers around the reins to indicate the horse should not move forwards. The instant the horse starts stepping backwards the fingers are relaxed. If required, the fingers can squeeze the reins alternately to cue the steps. Alternatively, the legs can be used to assist stepping. The horse is always ridden forwards after a rein-back.

RIDER TIP...

In rein-back the horse's forward energy is momentarily stopped by the seat and redirected backward via a new 'door' which is created by the legs.

STRAIGHTNESS, BEND, FLEXION AND CIRCLES

To produce a symmetrically muscled, athletic and supple horse the rider must focus on developing true bend and straightness. They are interdependent and complementary elements in training. The rider aims to develop both longitudinal and lateral suppleness. Longitudinal suppleness is reflected in the horse's adjustability and his ability to lengthen and shorten his stride. Lateral suppleness assists the horse in circling and bending his body and neck.

Training the horse to develop strength and suppleness when working on both reins is essential for the development of connection, throughness, straightness, impulsion, engagement and collection.

STRAIGHTNESS

Straightness is concerned with the development of equally strong and supple musculature on both sides of the horse. The development of equal thrust from the back legs assists the horse with his balance and in travelling in a straight line. Developing straightness is an ongoing process which continues throughout the horse's ridden life. The more athletically demanding the work, the more important straightness becomes as it can help to protect the horse from injury.

The focus with a newly backed horse is the development of 'travelling straight'. In nature horses do not naturally travel with straightness.

STRAIGHTNESS ASSISTS A HORSE BY OPTIMISING HIS FORWARD THRUST AND IMPULSION.

RIDER TIP...

When considering straightness it must be remembered that the horse is narrower in the shoulders than the hind quarters. The rider should focus on the alignment of the horse's spine.

LATERALITY

Laterality describes the preferential use of a diagonal limb pairing or of a specific limb. This can be observed when the horse performs a variety of actions such as pawing, striking and selecting a canter lead.

The preferential use of one diagonal pairing results in differences in the carrying and pushing power of his limbs. This creates asymmetries in limb movements and body position. As a result of laterality, most horses will bend more easily on one rein and will have a preferred canter lead.

RIDING CIRCLES

When riding a circle, the horse should balance his weight equally over the left and right sides, devoid of any inward leaning. Horses are initially trained on a larger circle, as performing smaller circles in balance requires greater strength.

The rider progressively trains the horse to use the outer forelimb to support the inner forelimb. This is the opposite of his natural tendency. When turning at speed, horses naturally lean to the inside, the inside forelimb bearing much of the forehand weight.

THE IMPORTANCE OF THE THORACIC SLING WHEN TURNING

The horse's ribcage is suspended between the forelimbs by means of a muscle sling, called the thoracic sling. The muscles are attached to the cervical vertebrae, the ribcage and behind the scapula. The Serratus ventralis thoracis muscle is the largest of the muscles which support the ribcage. It is comprised of 4 sections: 2 cervical (neck) and 2 thoracic (chest) sections. When a forelimb is lifted in movement, the muscles of the thoracic sling stabilise the ribcage and maintain horizontal balance. Equal strength in the left and right sling muscles must be developed to support the ribcage when the horse is circling.

When the sling muscles are engaged (contracted), the horse's withers lift. This results in the horse becoming physically taller; more importantly it enables the horse to travel with more uphill balance and to lighten his forehand. The lightened forehand is not only desirable for rider comfort, but it also renders the forehand more mobile, enabling more responsive changes of direction. When the sling muscles are relaxed, the withers are lower, and the horse travels in a less uphill manner. The muscle sling takes time to develop the strength to lift the additional weight of the rider.

BEND AND CIRCLES

Bend refers to flexing throughout the length of the horse from nose to tail. Bend can be subdivided into:

LONGITUDINAL BEND... refers to the topline of the horse.

LATERAL BEND... describes a curve from nose to tail either left or right.

It is often stated that, when circling, the horse must bend evenly from head to tail around the rider's inside leg. However, modern scientific studies have confirmed that the connections between the horse's vertebrae are not equally flexible.

THE HORSE'S SPINE IS INCAPABLE OF BENDING EVENLY FROM NOSE TO TAIL.

In dressage, the appearance of bend is desirable. Taller and longer-backed horses may appear to have more bend throughout their length than smaller and shorter-backed horses.

THE EQUINE SPINE

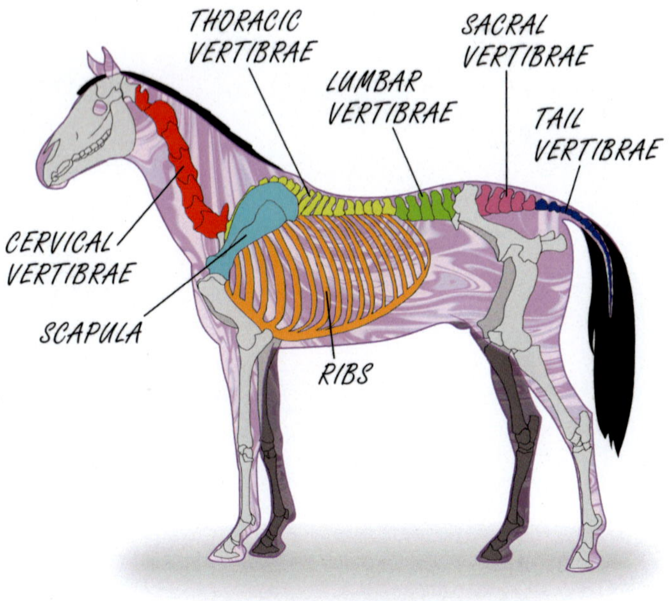

The equine spine consists of vertebrae and associated structures: long and short spinal ligaments; intrinsic and extrinsic spinal muscles, and structures related to articulation. Bend is achieved by vertebral movement in 3 dimensions. The degree to which the vertebral column can bend varies with the region of the spine and the type of rotation that is possible.

Horses have approximately 56 vertebrae; the number of thoracic or lumbar vertebrae may vary. This variation is generally compensated by a change in the number of vertebrae in an adjacent region. As a general rule, a horse has:

- 7 vertebrae in the neck region; C1 adjoins the skull and C7 at the base of the neck.
- 18 thoracic vertebrae, located at the withers and under the saddle area, T1 to T18.
- 6 lumbar vertebrae in the loin area behind the saddle, L1 to L6.
- 5 sacral vertebrae in the croup, S1 to S5.
- 20 vertebrae in the tail.

The vertebral column of the horse can move in 3 different ways: FLEXION-EXTENSION, LATERAL BENDING, and AXIAL ROTATION.

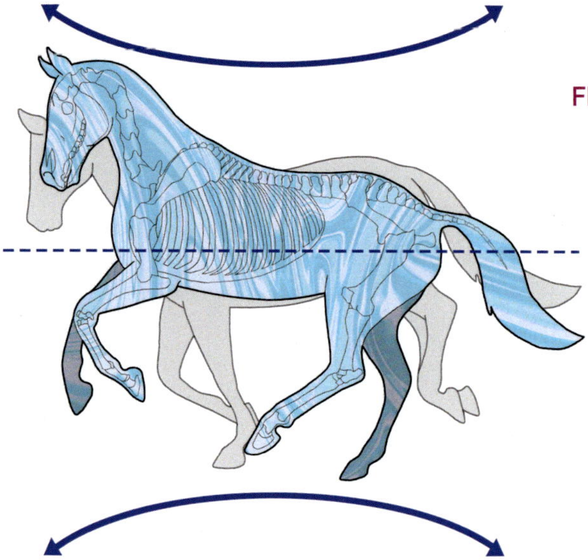

FLEXION EXTENSION

FLEXION-EXTENSION… of the spine permits LENGTHENING and SHORTENING of the horse's frame and ROUNDING or HOLLOWING of the back.

LATERAL BENDING… of the spine permits BENDING TO THE LEFT OR RIGHT.

AXIAL ROTATION… of the spine permits the vertebral column to TWIST.

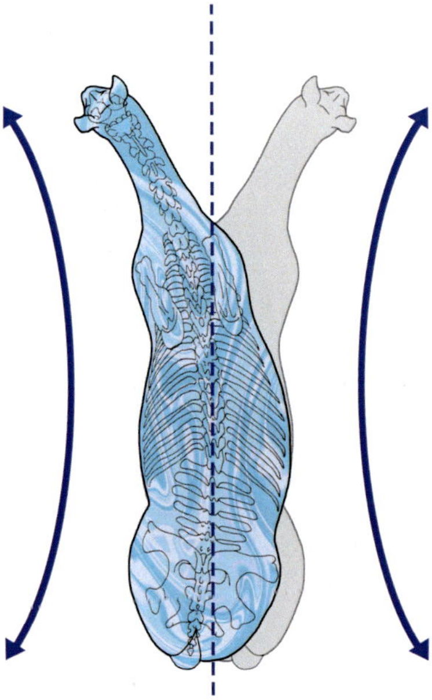

LATERAL BEND

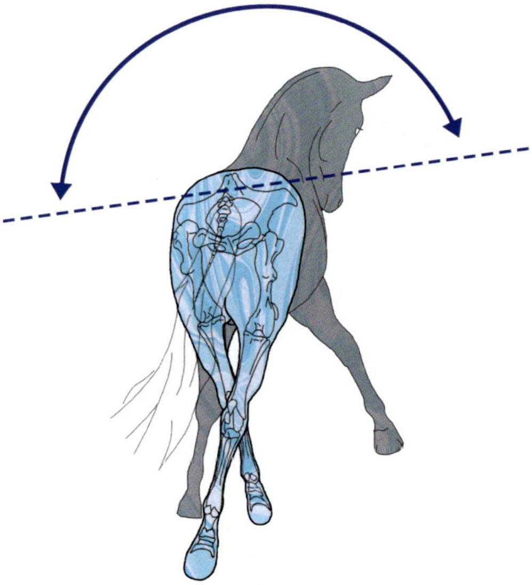

AXIAL ROTATION

Certain areas or joints in the vertebral column have much greater mobility than others. This results in variable mobility throughout the length of the horse and creates difficulty controlling bend. Horses can vary significantly in the amount of movement possible between vertebrae and therefore how much longitudinal and lateral bend they are capable of.

The cervical vertebrae in the head and neck region have the highest range of motion, allowing the horse mobility for grazing and self-grooming. Most of the neck movement occurs at the most flexible joint in the equine spine, the junction between C7 and T1. Horses tend to raise, lower, or turn the neck from its base rather than by equal movements throughout all the neck joints. Horses tending to overbend at the base of the neck when circling create difficulties for the rider.

Movement in the thoracic and lumber sections of the spine is relatively limited; however, considering the cumulative effect of a small amount of movement at each joint, some movement is possible. The range of motion in this region varies with the gait.

The five sacral vertebrae are completely rigid as their intervertebral discs are fused; this increases the effectiveness of the forward thrust from the hind limbs.

The vertebrae in the tail region have a good range of motion.

THE EQUINE RIBCAGE'S ROLE IN BEND

The equine ribcage has 18 pairs of ribs, each pair associated with the 18 thoracic vertebrae (T1 -T18). The first 8 pairs of ribs (termed true ribs) are directly attached, at the bottom to the sternum and at the top to the spine. As a result of this direct connection, they are not as mobile as the 10 'false ribs' located in the T9 to T18 area of the spine. The false ribs have spring which enables the chest to expand and contract as the horse breathes.

The horse is capable of pulling the ribs on the inside of the bend closer together whilst allowing the ribs on the outside to be stretched apart. Much of the bend observed on a circle is the result of the horse moving his ribcage towards the outside of the bend.

The appearance of bend throughout the length of the horse is further assisted by the positioning of the inside hindlimb and forelimb. The horse can move his legs close to his midline (adduction) and move them away from the midline (abduction).

THE AIDS FOR BEND

The aim is to achieve as even a bend as possible from nose to tail. Bend and flexion can be created by the rider's seat alone.

The main aid for bend is a weight aid using the inside seat bone which applies gentle sideways pressure on the ribcage, asking it to yield to the outside. The horse should yield to pressure from the rider's inside seatbone and her inside leg.

The rider's inside leg should become pillar-like by engaging the inside leg muscles to support the seat aid. The horse should 'bend around the leg'. The outside seatbone,

RIDER TIP...

The 'inside' refers to the inside of the movement.

RIDER TIP...

Allow bend with your outside rein.

and leg if necessary, should be placed forwards to indicate that the forehand should move towards the inside. The inside rein can indicate bend by closing and releasing the fingers or by gentle vibration. The contact should remain consistent. The inside rein should never be pulled backwards, causing the horse's outside hind to abduct and travel outside off the required track. A backwards pull on the inside rein creates too much movement between C7 and T1, at the base of the neck. The rider should turn her body from the waist. The outside arm and hand allow and control the amount of neck bend. The rider's shoulder positioning helps regulate the amount of bend and the position of the forehand.

The secret of creating a good bend is to apply the aids lightly. Strong aids will cause the horse to hold his ribcage tightly against the discomfort.

If the horse's outside hind abducts, the rider should correct this by moving their outside leg backwards and asking the quarters to move inwards.

RIDER TIP...

Avoid gripping with the legs as this will block the horse's ability to bend.

RIDER TIP...

Strong leg aids can cause a horse to hold his ribcage tensely, which will limit his ability to bend.

FLEXION

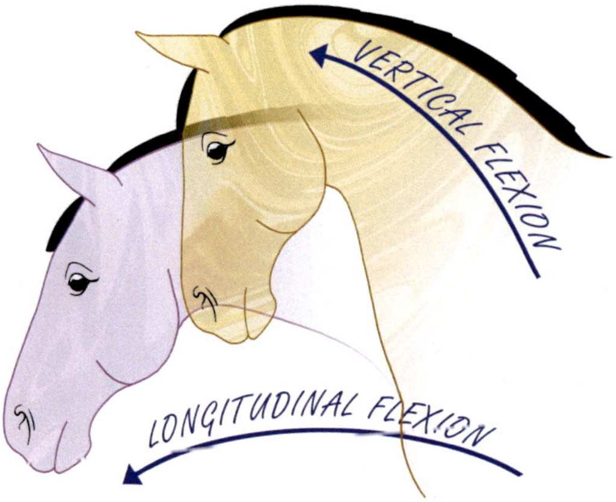

There are two types of flexion: lateral flexion and longitudinal flexion:

LATERAL FLEXION... describes the horse's head when it is positioned very slightly to the left or right with minimal neck bend.

LONGITUDINAL FLEXION... describes a softening and relaxation in the poll area which allows the horse's nose to relax towards the vertical.

The poll is a protrusion at the highest point of the equine skull and as such cannot relax or rotate. Many important tendons and muscles attach at the poll. When equestrians talk of relaxation at the poll

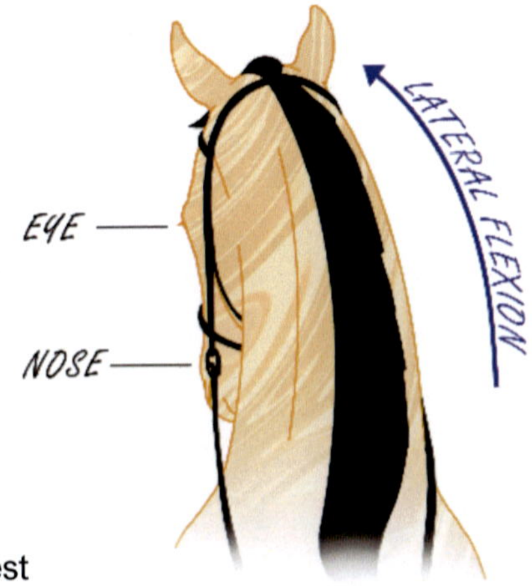

or flexion of the poll, they are in fact referring to the area behind the poll which consists of the first two vertebrae of the neck forming a curved ridge at the top of the neck.

Movement at the poll is dependent on the horse's ability to stretch the top area of his neck, the area where C1 (the atlas) and C2 (the axis) are located. A soft elastic contact enables the horse to flex in this area.

THE AID FOR LATERAL FLEXION

The aid for lateral flexion is the lightest and subtlest influence. The rider should engage slightly her inside seat bone, by dropping weight into her heel or by pressing lightly on the stirrup. The inside hand should close softly as if gently squeezing a damp sponge. The hand is then relaxed when the horse complies. The outside rein is used to limit the degree of flexion. The head should not tilt, and the ears should remain level; only the corner of the eye and the rim of the nostril should be visible to the rider.

THE AID FOR LONGITUDINAL FLEXION

The aid for longitudinal flexion is a gentle vibration of the rein. It is wise to start with the tiniest possible movement and build up to a level that results in the release of tension. The most effective way to achieve this is to vibrate the rein in which the rider feels slightly more tension. Small vibrations are more effective than large vibrations.

Longitudinal flexion is best achieved by riding with a light, giving contact. The horse should be allowed to stretch forward and release unnecessary tension at the top of his neck in the C1 and C2 area. The rider should have the feeling of the horse's neck lifting upwards and outwards of the chest, stretching forwards and around. No backward pull should be used.

YOU CANNOT BEND YOUR HORSE WITHOUT FLEXION BUT YOU CAN FLEX YOUR HORSE WITHOUT BENDING.

LATERAL WORK, TURNS, PIROUETTES AND FULL-PASS

A good outline and collection is achieved through correct training and the judicious use of exercises which improve self-carriage, longitudinal and lateral suppleness and improve a horse's symmetrical body balance. The importance of regular lateral work cannot be over- stated.

LATERAL WORK HAS MANY BENEFITS FOR THE HORSE...

- It improves his attentiveness to the aids.
- It improves his shoulder mobility.
- It improves the flexibility of his haunches.
- It strengthens the muscles of his thoracic sling.
- It improves his symmetrical body balance.
- It improves his balance, agility and manoeuvrability.
- It improves his longitudinal and lateral suppleness.
- It improves the quality of his bend, his straightness and suppleness.
- It improves his self-carriage.

LATERAL WORK HAS MANY BENEFITS FOR THE RIDER. IT CAN HELP HER...

- To refine her riding position.
- To obtain a more flexible seat.
- To finesse the use of her seat.
- To apply weight aids accurately.
- To improve the timing of her aids.
- To improve the timing of her half-halts.
- To finesse control of the direction of her activating aids.
- To improve the application of her outside aids.

- To improve the subtlety of her holding aids.
- To redirect the horse's movement without losing forwardness.
- To use sensitive aiding to retain good quality bend.

Lateral exercises should be gradually introduced into a training regime to allow the horse the necessary time to develop sufficient strength to perform them. The exercises require the repeated use of his leg adductor and abductor muscles which are rarely used when the horse is at liberty. It is easier to ride these movements in the slower paces and for this reason horses initially learn lateral work in walk and trot. These exercises require fine control of the balance and timing of the aids to assist the horse in retaining his balance. It is difficult to create bend throughout the horse's spine at speed. The greater the speed at which a horse travels the more rigidly he will hold his spine.

In lateral movements the horse uses the ground reaction forces differently when actioning the various lateral thrusts required. Lateral exercise requires the horse to reach further underneath his body with his hind legs and he achieves this by raising his back, increasing flexion of his hind legs and by a greater flexion of his lumbosacral joint. These lateral movements are often coupled with forward movement, the exceptions being turn on the forehand, turn on the haunches, full-pass and pirouettes.

IMPORTANT TIPS...

FORWARD MOVEMENT SHOULD ALWAYS TAKE PRECEDENCE OVER LATERAL MOVEMENT. THE MOMENT THE HORSE LOSES THIS THE RIDER SHOULD STRAIGHTEN HIM TO REGAIN HIS FORWARDNESS.

TO PERFORM THESE EXERCISES WELL, THE RIDER MUST BE CAPABLE OF ADVANCING EACH HIP INDEPENDENTLY. THIS CAN BE PRACTISED BY PLACING A HEAVY HARDBACK BOOK WITH AN OVERHANG ON A TABLE. NEXT STAND IN RIDING ALIGNMENT, LEGS APART, KNEES SOFTLY BENT WITH THE TOES A FEW INCHES BACK FROM THE TABLE EDGE, AND PUSH THE BOOK BACK ON TO THE TABLE BY ADVANCING EACH HIP INDEPENDENTLY. THE FEET MUST REMAIN GROUNDED, THE HEELS SHOULD NOT RISE.

TURN ON THE FOREHAND AND TURN ON THE HAUNCHES

The exercises teach the horse to respond to the rider's leg in a different way, i.e.to move away from the leg. These basic turns are introduced early in the horse's training, with turn on the forehand first to be introduced. These exercises have no collecting effects.

TURN ON THE FOREHAND

The turn on the forehand consists of a series of steps performed in walk. The horse begins the movement from a standstill and moves his quarters in a circle by pivoting around his inside front hoof. Importantly, to avoid damaging the inside foreleg, he must pick up and replace this hoof. This turn can be performed clockwise or anti-clockwise by moving the quarters 90 degrees (a quarter turn), 180 degrees (a half turn), 270 degrees (three quarters turn) or 360 degrees (a full turn).

THE AIDS FOR TURN ON THE FOREHAND

The aids for turn on the forehand commence with the rider placing a little more weight on her inside seatbone and asking for a slight flexion at the poll towards the inside of the turn. The rider indicates the direction of the turn with her inside rein whilst taking her inside leg backwards to ask the haunches to step away from her inside leg. Initially the rider's outside leg and seatbone should be relaxed and she must be careful not to block the movement by premature use of her controlling aids. The outside seatbone, leg and hand are used to control the size and speed of the steps. The rider's inside leg is not continually applied but is used to initiate each step. The horse should step rhythmically without stepping forwards. If the rider perceives that the horse is attempting to step forward she should momentarily close her hands to prevent this.

RIDER TIP...

The rider should not look downwards at the inside front hoof. She should retain good upper body alignment.

RIDER TIP...

Excessive use of the inside leg will cause the horse to move too hurriedly.

TURN ON THE HAUNCHES

The turn on the haunches is performed in walk. Although appearing similar to a walk pirouette, it differs in that it is not performed in a collected walk. The horse's forehand travels around the horse's inside hind leg by describing a circle. The inside hind leg must be lifted and replaced in rhythm with the walk step sequence. It can be performed clockwise or anticlockwise by moving the forehand 90 degrees (a quarter turn), 180 degrees (a half turn), 270 degrees (three quarters turn) or 360 degrees (a full turn).

THE AIDS FOR TURN ON THE HAUNCHES

To perform a turn on the haunches, the rider must coordinate several aids. The rider should place a little more weight on her inside seatbone and ask for slight flexion at the poll towards the inside of the turn. The rider indicates the direction of the turn with her inside rein whilst she asks the horse to bend around her inside leg. Her shoulders are positioned slightly behind vertical alignment to discourage forward movement.

When first introducing this movement to the horse, her outside leg and seatbone are slightly advanced to ask the horse's forehand to move laterally and to step around his

RIDER TIP...

Do not pull backwards or overuse the inside hand as this will cause the horse's haunches to swing away.

inside hind leg. The outside seatbone applies pressure in the direction of the turn. The outside leg initiates the steps. The outside rein allows and controls the bend and if necessary is used to prevent forward movement. The inside rein can be opened to help lead the forehand around the turn.

RIDER TIP...

The focus should be on maintaining active rhythmic steps and when first introduced it is acceptable for the hind hooves to make a small circle.

LEG-YIELD, SHOULDER-FORE AND COUNTER-SHOULDER-FORE

These exercises are initially performed on straight lines but once mastered they can be performed on curved lines, circles and through the corners of the arena.

LEG-YIELD

Leg-yield is normally performed in walk and trot. Leg-yield is initially introduced by asking the horse on approaching the corner to turn a few metres earlier down the long side of the arena and then asking him to proceed in leg-yield towards the outside track. The horse is normally inclined to move towards the outside track.

Leg-yield has suppling and strengthening effects. Its purpose is to teach the horse to move away from (to yield) subtle pressure from the rider's inside seat bone and lower leg. In leg-yield the horse's head, neck and body can be aligned or he may be flexed slightly away from the direction of travel. Initially the horse is asked to travel along a

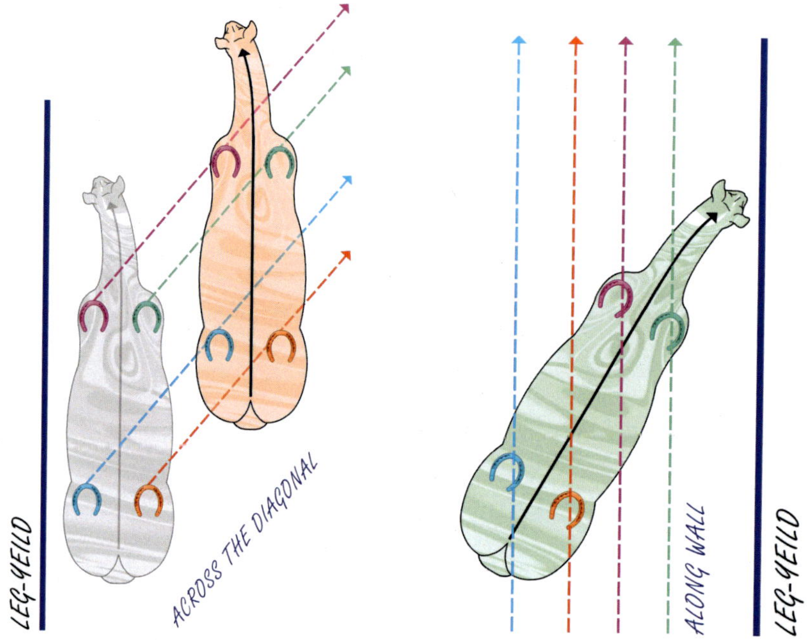

diagonal path, the direction of his steps being both forwards and to the side. The horse must cross his inside foreleg over his outside foreleg and his inside hind leg over his outside hind leg.

When the horse is proficient in stepping towards the track on both reins he is then asked to leg-yield towards the centre of the arena or across a diagonal. More advanced versions of leg-yield can be performed along the arena wall with either the horse's head or his quarters positioned nearest to the wall. Leg-yield can also be performed on a circle with either the horse's head or his quarters positioned towards the centre of the circle.

RIDER TIP...

Most horses are narrower in their shoulders than in their hind quarters. When riding leg-yield it is important to focus on the horse's spinal alignment rather than aligning either his outside hooves or his inside hooves.

THE AIDS FOR LEG-YIELD

When the rider is first taught leg-yield she is often advised to use a slight weighting of her inside seatbone; this is to assist her in using her seatbone in the direction of travel. Her inside leg should be moved back slightly to influence and assist the hind quarters in moving actively forwards and to the side. In this instance the horse's head and neck is slightly flexed away from the direction of travel as it is more difficult to leg-yield whilst keeping the horse's head and neck straight.

To influence the quarters, her inside seatbone and inside leg aids activate the steps. Her aids must be carefully timed, being applied as the horse's inside hind leg commences its stance phase. Her outside seatbone, leg and hand are used to control spinal straightness, to prevent the horse from falling out through his outside shoulder and to prevent him from rushing to avoid the activating aids. If required, her outside hand can be outwardly moved to direct the movement. If necessary, the aids may be repeated at every step.

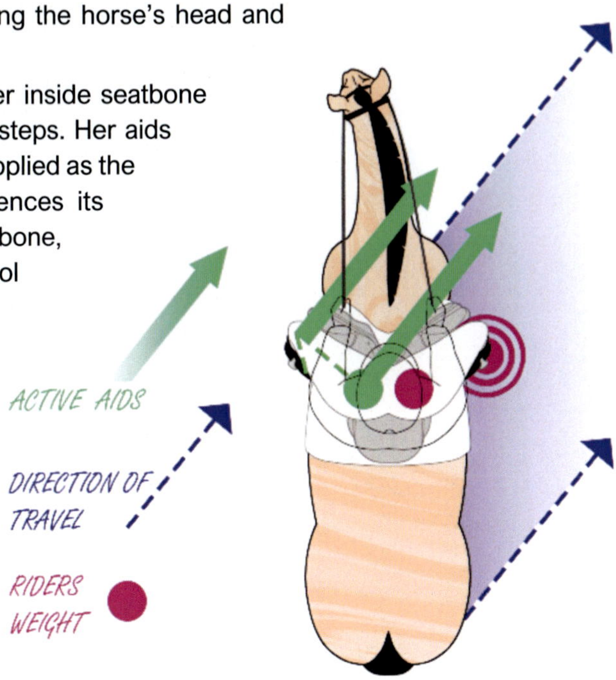

The more advanced rider leg-yields with the horse's head, neck and spine aligned. She is capable of using her weight aids and activating aids independently. She positions her outside leg off the horse's side and lightly weights her outside seatbone to move her centre of gravity towards the direction of travel. Note that if the rider places to much weight on the outside seatbone she will block the lateral movement. Her focus should be on assisting lateral movement by slightly adjusting her centre of gravity, enabling the horse to cover more ground laterally.

RIDER TIP…

Positioning the outside leg slightly off the horse's side indicates that you wish him to move in that direction.

RIDER TIP…

The outside rein may be moved away from the horse's neck to indicate the direction of travel.

SHOULDER-FORE AND COUNTER SHOULDER-FORE

Shoulder-fore and counter shoulder-fore are lesser versions of shoulder-in and counter shoulder-in. They are used to introduce the concept of shoulder-in to the novice horse or the novice rider. The horse is asked to bend around and move away from the inside leg and seatbone. These suppling exercises should create greater freedom in the horse's shoulders and enable him to develop greater engagement of his hind quarters. These exercises improve the horse's longitudinal and lateral suppleness. They are best performed early in a warm-up session to gently prepare the horse for the more advanced lateral exercises.

SHOULDER-FORE

Initially trained in walk to assist the rider in using her seatbones effectively, shoulder-fore can be performed in walk, trot or canter. The horse is asked to displace his forehand to the inside of the direction of travel. The hind quarters and hind feet should not change their initial direction of travel. The extent of this forehand displacement is dependent on his flexibility and how easily he can bend his lumbar and thoracic spine without adversely affecting his ability to rhythmically step under. The displacement of the forehand can range from 1 hoof's breadth to almost reaching the 3-track version of shoulder-in.

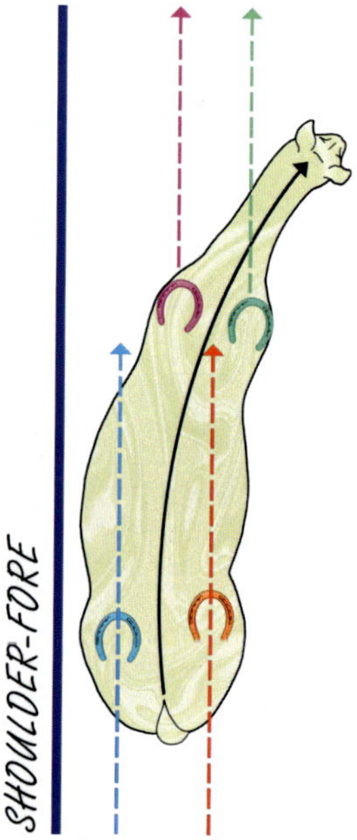

Shoulder-fore is initially performed along the long side of the arena. The horse's hind legs and back hooves should remain as if the horse were travelling in a straight line along the track. This exercise helps to improve the horse's balance and develops increased strength and greater weight-bearing upon his haunches. Shoulder-fore can be ridden through corners, on circles, through loops, up the centre line, and along the 5 metre lines.

THE AIDS FOR SHOULDER-FORE

As with any lateral exercise which requires the horse to bend through his lumbar and thoracic spine, the rider creates a bend before riding laterally. A large circle can be ridden in advance of this exercise to assist the creation of bend. In shoulder-fore the rider's waist, shoulders, hands, and head should be positioned as if riding a large circle. The key to creating good bend is the subtle application of the aids.

The aids for shoulder-fore are a lesser version of the aids used for shoulder-in. The rider creates lumbar and thoracic bend in the horse by lightly weighting her inside seatbone whilst applying gentle sideways pressure on the horse's ribcage to ask it to move towards the outside of the bend. To support her seat aid, her inside leg should become pillarlike. She achieves this by the engagement of the muscles of her inside leg in contact with the horse's side and linking them to the action of her inside seatbone. The inside rein can indicate bend by closing and releasing the fingers or by a gentle vibration. Importantly, the inside rein should never be pulled backwards creating excessive movement at the base of the horse's neck.

As she applies these aids and in order to avoid interrupting the flow of the horse's movement, her outside seatbone is advanced to ask the horse's outside shoulder to move inwards and she turns her body slightly towards the inside of the arena from the waist. In this moment she must be quick to action a half-halt to prevent the horse from travelling forwards in an arc. As her shoulders rotate slightly to the inside, her hands mirror this action enabling her contact to remain consistent. Her outside arm and hand should both allow and control the degree of neck bend. The rider's shoulder position helps to regulate the degree of bend and the position of his forehand and her shoulders should be parallel to the horse's shoulders at all times. Her inside leg is used to create impulsion and to assist the horse in moving laterally.

Her gaze should be positioned above and through the horse's ears. The seat and leg aids are applied in the direction of travel and should indicate that the horse should continue to travel laterally. Half-halts can be applied to keep the horse in the shoulder-fore orientation.

The rider's outside hand and rein can be used if necessary to prevent the horse from falling out through his outside shoulder. He should remain balanced, with his shoulders lifted and his steps rhythmical and energetic.

If his haunches start to swing out, the rider's outside leg can be used behind the girth to correct this.

RIDER TIP...

Direct your gaze above and between your horse's ears. Resist the temptation to look down at his shoulders.

RIDER TIP...

To encourage the horse to step further underneath himself, focus on feeling the horse's back lifting up under your seatbones.

If the horse loses rhythm or forwardness the rider should exit shoulder-fore either by riding forwards on a curve or she may straighten the horse by synchronously advancing her inside seatbone whilst retracting her outside seatbone.

RIDER TIP…

Do not apply the leg aids too powerfully as this stiffens your lower back, discouraging the horse from lifting his back under your seat.

RIDER TIP…

You may move your inside hand towards the midline of the horse's neck but you must keep your hands either side of it.

COUNTER SHOULDER-FORE

To perform this exercise the rider simply uses the aids which she uses for Shoulder-fore. The inside of any movement is the side to which the horse is bent or flexed. Counter shoulder-fore is the mirror image of shoulder-fore. The horse's head, neck and shoulders are positioned towards the outside of the arena. It is helpful to understand the exercise knowing that the horse's shoulders can only be bent either to the left or to the right. The term shoulder-fore and counter shoulder-fore are only applicable when performed in an arena or an enclosed space.

MORE ADVANCED LATERAL WORK

Horses vary significantly in their flexibility and some horses will find advanced lateral work harder than others. When first introduced the rider should be content with a few steps well performed, always ensuring that the horse's desire to move forwards is preserved. The exercises are not beneficial if the horse has lost activity.

More advanced lateral movements, shoulder-in, counter shoulder-in, haunches-in (travers) or haunches-out (renvers) are beneficial for the horse's physical development and will improve his flexibility, his collection, the quality of his gaits and his straightness. They can be developed within the walk, trot, or canter by moving either the horse's shoulders or his hips to one side of the track whilst bending his spine and engaging his inside hind leg underneath his body. However, as the horse finds it easier to bend away from the direction of travel, shoulder-in and counter shoulder-in are taught before travers, renvers and half-pass.

SHOULDER-IN

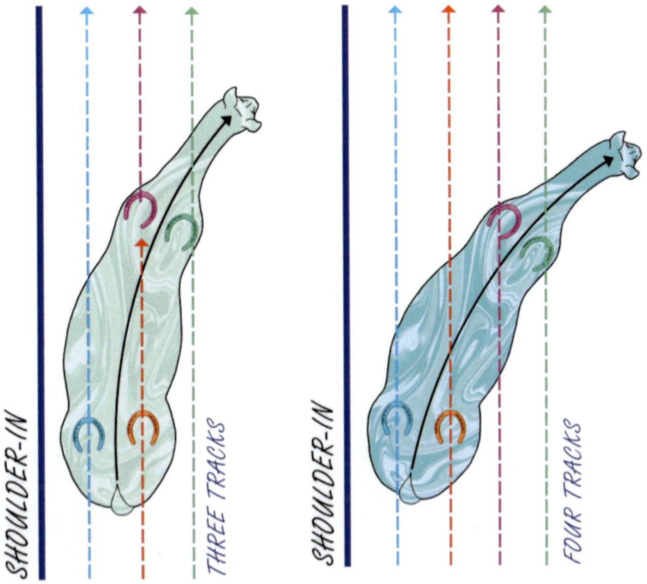

In shoulder-in the horse's shoulders are lifted and are bent towards the centre of the arena. The horse is bent to the inside of the movement around the rider's inside leg with his head positioned away from the direction of travel. His hind feet should remain on the track and the horse should bend through his thoracic and lumbar regions. His hind legs should remain travelling with straightness and should not cross over each other. The inside foreleg crosses and passes in front of the outside foreleg. The horse should bend without swinging out his haunches.

Historically shoulder-in was performed in 4-tracks which is more demanding for the horse than the 3-track option which is commonly practised today.

Shoulder-in increases the horse's lateral and longitudinal suppleness and this improves his straightness. It requires the horse to step further under his torso and is achieved by increased bending of the joints of his hind legs and increased bending of his lumbosacral joint.

It can be performed along straight lines, through turns and on circles.

The main purposes of this exercise are:

- To improve the range of the horse's shoulder movements and thereby to improve the quality of his gaits.
- To develop increased engagement of his hind quarters.
- To lighten the horse's forehand and render it more mobile.

3-TRACK SHOULDER-IN

As the name suggests, the horse's hooves should travel along three distinct tracks. The aim is that the outside foreleg and the inside hind should travel along the middle track with the outside hind and inside foreleg travelling along separate tracks. Shoulder-in can be ridden in walk, trot and canter.

4-TRACK SHOULDER-IN

The 4-track shoulder-in is a much more demanding exercise than the 3-track. It requires the horse to display far greater spinal flexibility and it is only trained in walk and trot. All 4 legs should travel along separate tracks. If the rider cannot maintain the horse's bend and control his quarters the exercise will revert to leg-yield.

THE AIDS FOR SHOULDER-IN

When first introduced to shoulder-in the horse should only be asked to perform the 3-track version of this exercise. The degree of bend required is similar to that when performing a 10 metre circle. For this reason, the novice horse is often asked to perform a 10 metre circle before commencing shoulder-in.

The aids used for shoulder-fore and shoulder-in are very similar, the difference being that the rider should ask the horse for more bend through his lumbar, thoracic and neck vertebrae in shoulder-in.

Shoulder-in is actioned by the rider lightly weighting her inside seatbone whilst using it to apply sideways pressure on the horse's ribcage to move it to the outside of the bend. To support her seat aid in creating bend her inside leg should become pillarlike. This is achieved by the engagement of the muscles of her inside leg in contact with the horse's side and linking them to the action of her inside seatbone. The inside rein can indicate bend by closing and releasing the fingers or by a gentle vibration. Importantly, the inside rein should never be pulled backwards creating excessive movement at the base of the horse's neck and causing his haunches to swing outwards.

RIDER TIP...

If the horse's hind feet do not travel close to straight alignment or if his quarters swing outwards, the horse does not have sufficient flexibility to perform the movement.

As she applies these aids and in order to avoid interference with the flow of the horse's movement, her outside seatbone is advanced to ask the horse's outside shoulder to move inwards, and she turns her body towards the inside of the arena from the waist. As her shoulders rotate to the inside her hands mirror this action and her contact remains consistent. When the horse's forehand is off the outside track and in 3-track alignment, a half-halt is used to prevent him from travelling forwards in an arc. The horse is then asked to move on a bias along three distinct tracks.

The rider's outside arm and hand should allow and control the degree of neck bend. The positioning of the rider's shoulders helps to regulate the bend and the position of his forehand. Her shoulders should be parallel to the horse's shoulders at all times, her inside leg used to create impulsion and to assist the horse in moving laterally.

RIDER TIP...

The horse will lose balance if hurried when performing advanced lateral exercises.

Her gaze should be positioned above and through the horse's ears with her aids indicating that he should continue to travel on a bias. Her inside seatbone and inside leg should apply aids which are timed to activate his inside hind leg. These seat and leg aids are applied in the direction of travel. Half-halts can be applied to keep the horse in shoulder-in orientation.

If she feels the horse losing impulsion, rhythm or forwardness the rider should exit shoulder-in. She can exit the movement by either riding forward on a curve across the arena or she can straighten the horse by synchronously advancing her inside seatbone whilst retracting her outside seatbone and moving her shoulders to ask the horse's shoulders to return to alignment.

When riding 4-track shoulder-in the horse requires a greater degree of spinal flexibility to perform the movement; once the rider has placed the forehand correctly off the track she may move her outside leg and seatbone back to control the quarters.

COUNTER SHOULDER-IN (OR SHOULDER-OUT)

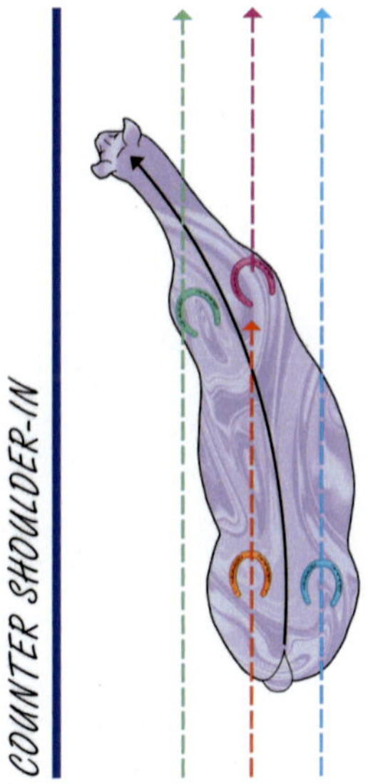

The terms shoulder-in and counter shoulder-in are only applicable when performed in an arena or an enclosed space. It is easier to understand this exercise if one considers that the horse's shoulders can only be bent to the left or to the right.

Counter shoulder-in is the counter movement of shoulder-in. The horse's haunches travel along an inner track and his shoulders are positioned to the outside of his body closer to the edge of the arena. The horse is bent away from the direction of travel. Counter shoulder-in can be thought of as being the mirror image of shoulder-in. It is somewhat harder for the rider to execute this exercise in the early phases of training as there is no outer wall to retain the positioning of the horse's haunches.

TRAVERS (HAUNCHES-IN)

Travers is a more difficult exercise than shoulders-in, requiring him to have developed greater spinal flexibility. The bend required to execute this exercise is similar to that required in a 6-metre volte.

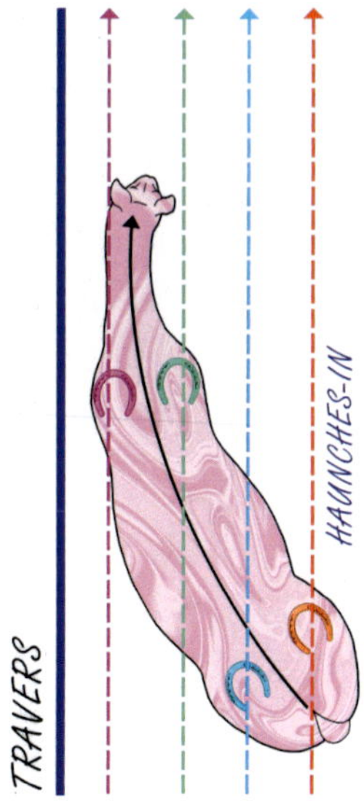

Travers is a 4-track exercise where the horse's shoulders and neck are straight and face the direction of travel. The horse's hind quarters are asked to travel along an inner path. The horse is bent around the rider's inside leg with a slight flexion of the poll to the inside. He can move his quarters inwards by moving his ribcage towards the outside of the bend and contracting the muscles which are situated behind the scapula and on the inside of his thoracic and lumbar spine whilst stretching and elongating the muscles situated towards the outside of the bend. Each of his 4 hooves should travel along a separate path. His outside hind leg should cross and travel in front of his inside hind leg. His forelegs should not cross and should remain as close to travelling with straightness as is possible.

As many horses tend to carry their quarters to one side, haunches-in and haunches-out are useful exercises to improve straightness as they strengthen the muscles in the horse's lumbar area and hind quarters.

RIDER TIP...

Be careful when using your outside leg that your weight aids remain on the inside of the movement.

THE AIDS FOR TRAVERS (HAUNCHES-IN)

The concept of travers is introduced to the horse from a circle; when a good quality bend has been established he is then asked to displace his quarters to the inside.

All advanced exercises can be broken down into simple components. To ride travers, the rider follows the same simple aiding rules that she has established throughout the horse's earlier training. As the inside of any movement is the inside of the bend, she weights her inside seatbone whilst using it to apply sideways pressure on the horse's ribcage to move it to the outside of the bend. To support her seat in creating this bend her inside leg should become pillarlike. As greater bend is required in this movement she must ask the horse to bend more tightly around her leg. Her inside leg not only creates bend but is also responsible for the creation of impulsion. The outside leg and seatbone are moved backwards to position the horse's haunches to the inside and the rider's outside leg should influence the horse's outside hind leg to ask him to step and cross over his inside hind.

RENVERS (HAUNCHES-OUT)

Renvers and travers are mirror images of each other. Renvers is a 4-track exercise which is considered harder to perform than its counter movement travers. When riding renvers the horse's shoulders travel in a straight line along a path a few metres in from the outer track with his haunches nearer to the arena wall. The horse should bend around the rider's inside leg with a slight flexion of the poll to the inside. His outside hind leg should cross and travel in front of his inside hind leg. His forelegs should not cross and should remain as close to travelling in straightness as is possible.

The terms renvers and travers are only applicable when performed in an arena or an enclosed space.

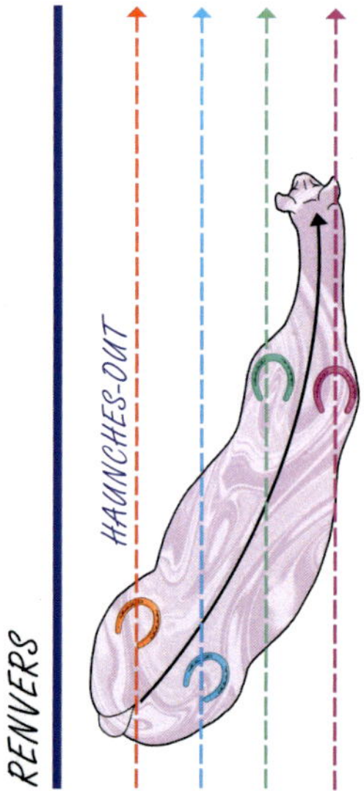

FULL-PASS

In full-pass the horse's movement is restricted to that of moving to the side. Its origins lie in military training with its original purpose being to permit riders in a line to space out evenly. It can be used in training to assist the rider to gain independent control of the horse's legs and to help her to refine her ability to isolate her aids and to use them independently. The horse's outside hooves are positioned just ahead of his inside hooves. Both the inside and the outside hooves should then travel along independent parallel lines. This manoeuvre is ridden along 4 tracks, the hooves of the forehand travelling in close proximity, as do the hooves of the hind limbs.

Full-pass is a good suppling and strengthening exercise, the horse using his leg adductor and abductor muscles to facilitate the side steps.

The full-pass should be commenced from a standstill rather than a square halt. Difficulties are created for the horse if the rider attempts this manoeuvre from a square halt, as his outside legs must step over the inside legs (the 'inside' being the direction of travel). The horse moves to the side without stepping forwards. Initially the full-pass is taught in walk and generally only practised in walk. Some very well trained horses can full-pass in trot and canter.

THE AIDS FOR FULL-PASS

When introducing full-pass, the rider's inside hand can indicate the direction of travel by moving it slightly away from the neck. The rider should ask for a slight flexion of the poll in the direction of travel which is created by the rider's inside leg and inside seatbone. The rider should place a little more weight on her inside seatbone. She should move her centre of gravity slightly towards the direction of travel. Her outside leg and outside seatbone asks the horse's outside legs to step over his inside legs.

The outside rein and the actions of her seat should prevent forward movement and the rider must not allow any backward movement. To complete the full-pass the rider ceases the use of her outside leg and seatbone and stops the movement by using her inside leg and seatbone.

RIDER TIP...

Be aware of your weight aid. Do not allow it to slip to the outside of the movement as this will unbalance the horse.

RIDER TIP...

A pole can be placed in front of the horse and used as a guide.

RIDER TIP...

The rider must be clear in her communication of the direction component of her aids.

HALF-PASS

Half-pass can be performed in collected walk, collected trot, collected canter and passage. It is not advisable to train half-pass until the horse is established in shoulder-in and travers. In half-pass his outside legs pass and cross in front of his inside legs. It is ridden across the arena at a 45 degree angle. The horse's poll should be flexed towards the direction of travel, and he should be bent round the rider's inside leg to assist his shoulder mobility. Importantly the forehand should precede the hind quarters. The horse should move gracefully, in balance and his steps should be expressive.

PIROUETTES

Pirouettes are advanced lateral movements in which the horse remains largely on the spot, performing a circle of 360 degrees by moving the forehand around the haunches which can be ridden in collected walk, collected canter and piaffe. Horses may perform quarter-pirouettes, half-pirouettes and more than one full pirouette. When first introduced to the horse it is acceptable for his quarters to move around a small circle.

EQUESTRIAN LANGUAGE

Equestrians have their own language. Many of the words and phrases used have evolved to enable a shortened form of communication with which to assist riders under instruction. Very often the words used rely on a detailed understanding of other riding concepts.

ABOVE THE BIT... describes the situation in which a horse carries his head and neck overly high in an attempt to avoid bit pressure.

ABDUCTION... the movement of a limb away from the midline of the body. The opposite of abduction is adduction.

ACCEPTING THE AIDS... a term used when a horse responds to the rider's requests without resistances or evasions.

ACCEPTING THE CONTACT... describes a horse that is accepting of the connection between the rider's hands and his mouth via the reins and bit.

ACCEPTING THE LEG... describes a horse that responds without resistance to aids given by the rider's leg.

ACTIVITY... describes the energy with which a horse is moving and responding to the aids.

ADDUCTION... describes the movement of a limb closer to the midline of the body. Abduction is the opposite of adduction.

AGAINST THE HAND... describes a horse that is leaning on or applying pressure against the rider's hand.

AIDS... the means by which a rider guides and influences the horse. They are subdivided as either Active or Passive aids. The Active aids can be Natural or Artificial.

BACKING UP... the action of moving the horse backwards either in-hand or under-saddle.

BALANCE... There are three aspects to balance in equestrianism. The first of these is rider balance. The second is the horse's balance. The third is the horse and rider moving in harmony in balance.

The horse's balance can be subdivided into lateral balance and longitudinal balance: LATERAL BALANCE refers to the relative distribution of the horse's weight over his left and right sides. LONGITUDINAL BALANCE (also known as horizontal balance) refers to the relative distribution of the horse's weight over his forehand and haunches.

BEHIND THE BIT... describes a horse that has pulled his nose in towards his chest in an attempt to avoid bit pressure.

BEHIND THE LEG... describes a horse that does not actively respond to the leg aids.

BEHIND THE VERTICAL (BTV)... describes the horse's head position in which his nose is carried near to his chest and behind an imaginary vertical line drawn from the browband to the ground.

BEND... describes the flexing of the horse from nose to tail. It is subdivided into longitudinal bend and lateral bend: LONGITUDINAL BEND refers to the flexing of the horse's topline. LATERAL BEND describes the curve which can occur from nose to tail either to the left or to the right.

BLOCKING... a riding position which blocks and hinders the horse's movement.

BIOMECHANICS... is the science of movement of a living body.

CADENCE... describes an elegant, balanced, rhythmic trot or canter. The steps of the gait are fluid, free of any restriction, with enhanced lifting and landing.

CANTLE... is the raised rear part of a saddle.

CANTER... is a three beat gait.

COLLECTION... The horse's frame is shortened as a result of increased engagement of the hindquarters and a greater arching and lifting of his back. The impression is given of the haunches bearing greater weight with the forehand elevated, the neck arched and carried high. The walk, trot, and canter can all be collected, the steps are elevated with shortened stride length.

CONFORMATION... is the shape or structure of an animal. A horse's conformation can be judged with reference to his intended use.

CONNECTION... describes a state where horse and rider are unified, are connected and are working as one. The rider should feel that the horse's hindquarters are elastically connected with the forehand. The horse is thereby responsive to subtle changes in the riding position.

CONTACT... describes the connection between the rider's hands and the horse's mouth via the reins and bit.

CORRECT DIAGONAL... when trotting a horse moves its legs as diagonal pairs, a moment of suspension occurring between each pairing. The left hind leg is paired with the right front leg and the right hind leg is paired with the left front leg. When in rising trot the rider should commence rising at the moment the horse's outside shoulder begins traveling forwards. This is termed 'rising on the correct diagonal'.

COUNTER-BENDING... counter-bending occurs when the bend is towards the outside rein. Normally the ridden horse is bent to varying degrees towards the inside rein when circling and turning.

COUNTER-CANTER... occurs when a horse leads the canter with the outside front leg as opposed to the inside front leg.

COUNTER-FLEXION... occurs when the horse is flexed to the outside at the poll.

COUNTER SHOULDER-IN... is a lateral movement in which the horse travels both forwards and to the side with the lateral bend towards the outside.

DEEP SEAT... describes a seat which remains in close contact with the saddle at all times.

DISENGAGED... refers to a horse that has lost the athletic connection between the hindquarters and his forehand.

DISUNITED CANTER... the second beat of the canter is normally a diagonal pairing. In the disunited canter the second beat is replaced by a lateral pairing.

ENGAGEMENT... this occurs as a result of the horse fluidly coordinating the flexion of his lumbosacral joint and his hind legs to position them further underneath a lifted back thus enabling the powerful propulsive use of his hindquarters.

EVASIONS... describes misbehaviours which are more severe than resistances, such as napping, bucking, spinning, stopping, and rearing.

EVADING THE CONTACT... describes a horse unwilling to accept the rein contact that is offered.

FALLING IN... occurs when a horse travels to the inside of the intended path.

FALLING IN THROUGH THE SHOULDER... occurs when a horse drifts to the inside of the intended path via his shoulder area.

FALLING OUT... occurs when a horse travels to the outside of the intended path.

FALLING OUT THROUGH THE SHOULDER... occurs when a horse drifts to the outside of the intended path via his shoulder area.

FEEL IN RIDING... describes the rider's ability to predict and react to the horse's actions.

FLEXION... describes the ability of a horse to bend either longitudinally or laterally at the poll. **LONGITUDINAL FLEXION** describes the softening and stretching of the muscles and associated structures at the poll which allow the nose to drop towards the vertical. **LATERAL FLEXION** describes the slight positioning of the horse's head to the left or right. This should be achieved by relaxation at the poll.

FLUIDITY... describes the horse's movement which is rhythmical, supple, and freely flowing forwards without constraint.

FORWARDNESS... describes the horse's desire and willingness to travel forwards in balance whilst working through into the rider's contact.

FRAMING THE HORSE... describes the use of the riding position and the passive aids to support the horse and to retain his straightness and his balance. This phrase should not be confused with 'putting the horse into a frame'.

FULL-PASS (or Full Travers)... is a movement in which the horse moves to the side only. Its origins lie in military training, its purpose is to assist riders in a line to space out evenly.

GROUND REACTION FORCE (GRF)... is the force which assists the horse to move. As the horse's hooves push against the ground, the GRF is the force of the ground reacting against the hoof.

HALF-HALT... a hardly visible, moderated version of the halt which increases the horse's balance and attentiveness. It is used to assist the hindquarters in becoming more engaged, to create impulsion and to lighten the forehand.

HALF-PASS... a lateral movement, a variation of travers, which is ridden on a diagonal line.

HAUNCHES-IN (or Travers)... a lateral movement in which the horse is bent in the direction of movement with his forehand on the track and his quarters inwardly positioned.

HAUNCHES-OUT (or Renvers)... a lateral movement, the counter movement to haunches-in. The horse is bent in the direction of movement towards the outside of the arena with the shoulders traveling on an inside track and the hindquarters outwardly positioned.

HYOID APPARATUS... the anatomical collective term for the bones which suspend the tongue and larynx. It is situated under the lower jawbone and in front of the upper spine. It is directly attached to the horse's tongue, the larynx, and the cervical spine.

HYPER-REACTIVE... a highly aroused state in which a horse responds excessively.

IMPULSION... a horse's ability to work forwards with controlled energy and power.

INDEPENDENT HANDS... describes a rider's hands when they are capable of influencing the horse independently of each other and are unaffected by the rider's movements.

INDEPENDENT SEAT... describes a seat that is sufficiently strong and flexible to action aids independently without adversely affecting riding position.

IN FRONT OF THE VERTICAL (IFV)... describes the horse's head position when his nose is carried ahead of an imaginary vertical line drawn from the browband to the ground.

IN FRONT OF THE LEG... describes a horse which moves freely forwards from light, subtle leg aids.

ISCHIUM... is the anatomical name for a seatbone (plural is ischia).

LATERAL BALANCE... describes the relative distribution of weight over the horse's left and right sides.

LATERAL WORK... describes movements in which the horse moves to the side. Lateral movement is usually coupled with forward movement with the exception of full-pass and pirouettes.

LEANING ON THE HANDS... describes a horse that uses the rider's hand to support the weight of his head and neck.

LEG-YIELD... is a lateral movement in which the horse travels both forwards and to the side, his inside legs passing and crossing in front of his outside legs.

LIGHTENED FOREHAND... through correct training the horse is able to lift his rib cage and transfer his centre of gravity towards his hindquarters, giving the rider the feeling of an uphill ride.

LONGITUDINAL BALANCE... the relative distribution of weight over the horse's forehand and haunches.

MISBEHAVIOURS... unwelcome and potentially dangerous behaviours such as rearing, bucking, or spinning.

NATURAL AIDS... are the aids the rider gives using different parts of her body. The voice is included in this category.

NATURAL OUTLINE... refers to the shape of the horse's silhouette from nose to tail when unrestrained.

ON THE BIT... describes a horse that has reached a fairly advanced level of training, is engaged, supple, connected, and working through from behind.

ON THE CONTACT... describes a horse that is accepting of an elastic connection with the rider's hands.

ON THE FOREHAND... describes a horse with poor longitudinal balance who is carrying an inappropriate amount of weight over his shoulders and front legs.

ON THE VERTICAL (OTV)... describes the horse's head position when it is aligned to an imaginary vertical line from the browband to the ground.

OUTLINE... describes the shape of the horse's silhouette from nose to tail.

OVER-BENT... describes a horse that is travelling with his nose behind the vertical and close to his chest.

PASSAGE... a very collected, slow, elevated, and cadenced trot. It is distinguished from a collected trot by its shorter stride length, slower and heightened steps and a more accentuated flexion of the knees and hocks. The stance phases and the periods of suspension are longer than that observed in collected trot.

PIAFFE... a highly collected diagonal movement performed on the spot. The haunches should be significantly lowered, with the hind feet well under the body. The limbs pause momentarily at their position of maximal height, but due to the lack of a suspension phase, it is technically not a trot.

PIROUETTE... an advanced lateral movement in which the horse remains largely on the spot, performing a circle of 360 degrees by moving the forehand around the haunches. Horses may perform quarter-pirouettes and half-pirouettes.

POLL... the poll of the horse is the highest point of the skull. Equestrians when referring to relaxation at the poll are in fact referring to the area behind the poll.

POMMEL... is the frontal upper part of a saddle.

PROTRACTION... describes the forwards swing of the horse's legs.

REIN-BACK... is a rearward diagonal movement with a two-beat rhythm.

RELAXATION... refers to both the physical and mental relaxation of the horse.

RENVERS (or Haunches-out)... is a lateral movement, the counter movement to haunches-in. The horse is bent in the direction of movement towards the outside of the arena with the shoulders travelling on an inside track and the hindquarters positioned to the outside.

RESISTANCE... an outdated term, it infers that the horse is unwilling to comply with a rider's requests.

RETRACTION… describes the backwards swing of the horse's legs.

RHYTHM… is the regular repeated pattern of movements and gaits.

RIDING ON A LOOSE REIN… describes riding with no contact, the reins forming loops allowing the horse to stretch his head, neck and topline.

RUNNING THROUGH THE HANDS… describes a horse that is unresponsive to light, slowing requests from the rider's hands.

SELF-CARRIAGE… moving in a self-maintaining, balanced and rhythmical way.

SHOULDER-FORE… is a moderated version of shoulder-in.

SHOULDER-IN… is a lateral movement in which the horse travels both forwards and to the side whilst maintaining a lateral bend to the inside.

STRAIGHTNESS… is a training goal. The horse having first developed equally impulsive hindquarters and strong, supple musculature throughout his body can move fluidly in balance.

SUPPLENESS… refers to the horse's ability to bend and move fluidly without stiffness. Suppleness can be subdivided into longitudinal suppleness and lateral suppleness. **LONGITUDINAL SUPPLENESS** describes the horse's adjustability, his ability to lengthen and shorten his frame and stride. **LATERAL SUPPLENESS** refers to the horse's ability to bend through his spine from nose to tail.

TACT… tact involves being sensitive to a horse's mental and physical welfare and is based upon a deep understanding of horse training practices, riding theory and the nature of horses.

TENSION… refers to excessive physical or mental tension in the horse.

TEMPO… refers to the rate at which the rhythm of a gait is repeated.

THE LUMBOSACRAL JOINT… a hinge joint and the third most flexible joint in the equine spine. It is located between the last lumbar vertebra and the first sacral vertebra.

THE THORACIC SLING… the term used for a group of muscles which support the horse's ribcage between his forelimbs.

THE SEAT… describes the rider's weight-bearing area which is in contact with the saddle.

THE VERTICAL… describes an imaginary vertical line which can be drawn from the browband to the ground.

THROUGHNESS... describes a level of connection between horse and rider which is more than 'connected'. A horse that is through is willing, relaxed, and accepting of the rider's aids, free from tension and resistance. The rider can direct the flow of the horse's energy both from back to front and from front to back.

TILTING... the horse's or rider's head when tipped to one side.

TIPPING... describes a rider with their upper body inclined forwards to the point that it negatively impacts balance.

TOPLINE... refers to the muscle groups that run along a horse's spine from the poll to the hindquarters.

TRACKING UP... describes the positioning of the horse's footfalls relative to each other. The horse's hind hooves should land on the imprints left by his front hooves when tracking up.

TRANSITION... describes a change from one movement to another.

TRANSITIONS WITHIN THE GAIT... occur when the rider asks the horse to change from one form of a gait to another. For example, in trot a horse can transition between collected, working, medium and extended trot.

TRAVELLING STRAIGHT... describes when the footfalls of a horse's hindquarters approximately land where his front feet had previously been placed.

TRAVERS (or Haunches-in)... is a lateral movement in which the horse is bent in the direction of movement with his forehand on the track and his quarters positioned inwards.

UP AT THE WITHERS... describes a horse which has contracted the muscles of his thoracic sling causing his ribcage to rise relative to his shoulder blades resulting in his withers being positioned higher.

UPWARDS TRANSITIONS... describes changing from a slower pace to a faster pace.

VOLTE... is a small circle of less than 10 metres in diameter.

ABOUT LYNNE BARRY

Lynne is a professional artist and teaches art. Art is in her blood – her mother is a professional artist and lecturer in art, her grandmother and her great grandmother were also artists. Lynne's sister is a professional graphic designer with her own agency, and her daughter is also a graphic designer.

Lynne spent her early childhood running barefoot in the South African bushveld, taking inspiration for her art from the beauty of the landscape, the wildlife and the exotic birds and plants. She does not remember a time when she did not paint.

Lynne has been involved in many equestrian disciplines and has competed successfully in Showing and Dressage. She has taught riding skills to beginners. Her favourite breed of horse is the Arabian. Her dream of owning an Arabian came true when she was gifted an Arabian mare called Mount Shar Shar's Beryl. After her daughter took over the ride on Beryl, Lynne purchased a 2-year-old Arabian gelding, Illizwe Sabre Dancer, which she produced and competed successfully.

Lynne is happiest when painting animals. She feels a deep connection to animals and is especially captivated by the horse's movement, his grace, his power, his beauty, his intelligence and his gentleness. She enjoys painting traditional animal portraits and lets her creative juices flow when she produces her fluid poured paint artworks. Alchemy is the best description of her fluid artworks; which show great skill in capturing and describing the essence, the spirt, the soul, the energy, the personality and the fluidity of the movement of the subject. Her artworks capture much more than a simple physical resemblance.

In addition to working with oil and acrylic paints, Lynne works in pencil, charcoal and watercolours.

Lynne exhibits her work regularly in South Africa and will take on private commissions. She also teaches art and illustrates books.

Lynne would like to thank the following photographers who allowed her to use their work as reference material :

Hillary O'Leary… 'Colourful'.

Kerry Afford… 'You can take a horse to water… but you can't make it drink'.

Karen Bloemmelsick… 'Corazon'.

Lynne can be contacted via:

E-mail… lynnebarryart@gmail.com

Instagram… lynnegeyl

Facebook… https://facebook.com/lynne.barry.77

LIST OF ARTWORKS BY LYNNE BARRY

"Gentle soul of Golde" Lynne Barry

ABOUT JENNIFER PELOSI

Jennifer Pelosi, grew up in Edinburgh and is currently living south of Edinburgh with her husband and young family. She has worked within the Architectural Industry for 20 years in the fields of technical drawing and 3D Visualisation.

She is a self-taught fine art pet portrait artist and hobby photographer specialising in horses and dogs.

Jennifer is a keen rider and has owned a few ponies; her latest is Mali, a Welsh Section D mare. Jen has competed in Showing and Dressage. Once her young family is more independent, Jennifer would like to work on her riding and to return to her fine art pet portraits and book illustrating.

Jennifer can be contacted via email: jenpelosi79@gmail.com

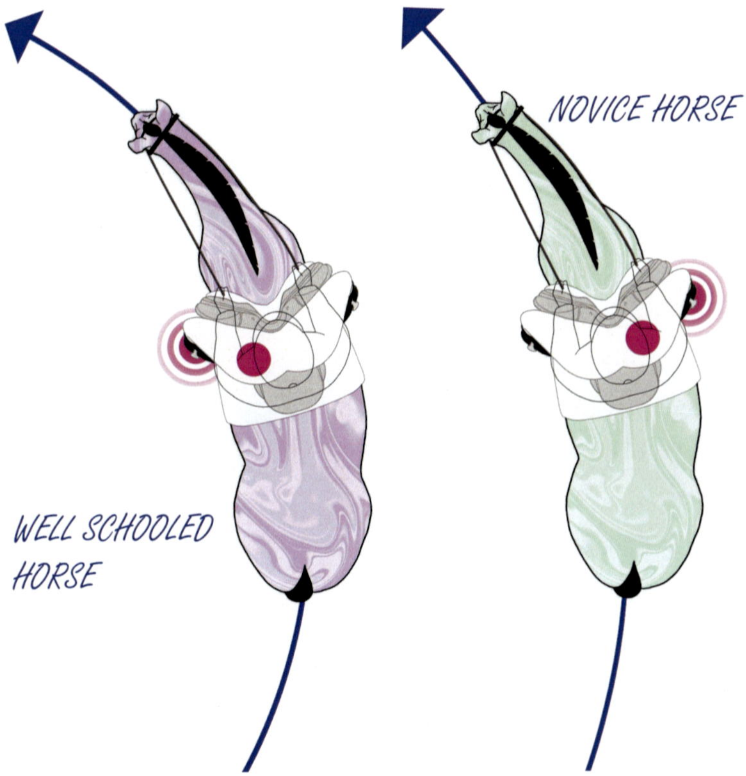
NOVICE HORSE
WELL SCHOOLED HORSE

LIST OF TECHNICAL ILLUSTRATIONS BY JENNIFER PELOSI

> "If a rider is in the correct position, and the horse was magically removed, they should land on their feet with their knees softly bent."
> Robert Hall

THE FAMILY

ROBERT NIGEL HALL FBHS

Born in Yorkshire 1927, Robert Hall became a world recognised and respected Dressage Trainer. He was the British Olympic Eventing Team's Dressage Trainer for Stockholm 1956, Rome 1960, and trainer for the British Olympic Dressage team in Tokyo 1964, and Mexico 1968. Robert Hall established three riding schools in the UK in which he taught his system, The Fulmer System, based on that established in the Spanish Riding School of Vienna.

Robert Hall inspired and taught a great many riders around the world. He was a man who had a genuine empathy for horses, an easy smile, and a good sense of humour. He was a passionate advocate of the horse, who had a gift for teaching equitation. His enthusiasm was infectious, and he generously shared his knowledge. He was happy to answer any and every question, giving reasons for his methods and detailed explanations as to why a certain combination or order of aids would work better than another.

Robert had the utmost respect for the horse, believing that the rider should only make reasonable requests of the horse and that riding should be a two-way process which involved having '*a conversation*'. The rider makes a request; the horse responds to it and this in turn determines how the rider will respond. He encouraged riders to develop 'feel', to listen to the horse, and to be *'aware that the horse is able to ask questions and make requests'*. Self-carriage was the goal and he cautioned that it could never be achieved by force.

He believed that the key to riding the more advanced movements was to *'get the basics right'*, the ultimate aim of the rider to achieve a picture in which the horse appeared to be moving unaided, purely for the joy of his movement.

In the 1980s, Robert moved to Aiken, South Carolina, America and settled on a 65-acre farm in Hitchcock Woods. Sadly, he did not write a book detailing his training system and insights.

I still clearly remember many of Robert's sayings and explanations and regularly quote my favourite ones. If you are lucky to find a great teacher like Robert Hall, his wisdom will stay with you throughout your riding years and if you are very lucky you will 'hear' him informing you as you ride.

MY BOOKS

There are two complementary books which are supported by a number of practical lesson-based workbooks.

My present book examines the form and function of the riding position with the aim of enhancing rider elegance and creating harmony. It details the theory of the aids, the techniques of their application and offers insights into how they can be refined to improve clearer communication and unify horse and rider.

My second book is a guide to ethical riding and training techniques. Its focus is on understanding which methods work best for the horse by considering the horse's nature, his natural biomechanics, intelligence, memory capacity and the processes by which he can learn.

Supporting these will be a number of lesson-based workbooks for riders. Each book will contain a variety of targeted lessons aimed at the improvement of rider techniques and feel. Each lesson will have a themed focus with detailed notes on how to perform the exercises and detailed descriptions of what the rider should 'feel'.